Touching the Heart of GOD

Ernest J. Gruen

586

TOUCHING THE HEART OF GOD

Ernest J. Gruen

Copyright © 1986 by Ernest J. Gruen.
Printed in the United States of America
ISBN: 0-88368-175-7

Edited by David L. Young

DEDICATION

This book is dedicated to the staff of *Full Faith Church of Love*. God has surrounded me with men and women who sincerely desire to make this ministry a success and a glory to God.

IN APPRECIATION

I genuinely wish to thank all the many sisters in our church who gave hours of their personal time in typing this manuscript: Penny Willis, Becky Emmerich, Jackie Janson, Iris Dyer, Karen Durden, Ruth Fox, Syd Stevens, Jan Carter, Laurie Johnson, Teresa Wright, Suzy Herd, and Mary Rafter.

In particular, I wish to thank Sue Baird, Nora Clements, Tricia Collier, Toni Arzola, and Kathy Reno for putting forth a concentrated effort to meet the final deadline.

A very special note of appreciation and gratitude to Mr. Dan Weddle for his expertise in transforming the spoken word into printed form with proper grammar and continuity.

I am deeply indebted to my personal secretary, Rose Davidson. It was her love for this book that caused it to be completed. Without her diligence, the book would have remained unfinished. Words cannot express my appreciation for her faithfulness.

CONTENTS

FOREWORD

In recent years we've experienced several "moves" of God—special emphases birthed by the Holy Spirit. While it has certainly been God's desire from creation that all men pray, recently something different has happened. The Holy Spirit has been sweeping all over the world, placing a "prayer desire" in the hearts of Christians everywhere.

Everywhere I have traveled across the globe I've discovered early morning prayer meetings—some of them meeting before dawn on a daily basis with thousands in attendance. Individuals are taking their vacations to pray, and families are praying together.

Many church leaders are withdrawing—some for long periods of time—to spend time in solitary prayer. Yonggi Cho has built a church in Seoul, Korea, of more than 500,000 members around his "Fasting-Prayer Mountain." Tens of thousands of people go there every day of the year to pray. Prayer retreats—both Catholic and Protestant— are springing up everywhere.

God provides the motivation. In turn He has commissioned Ernie Gruen, a man of prayer, to tell us how. Read expectantly. Prayerfully. Ernie's book will not change your life, but prayer will. His book, however, will show you how it's done.

Jamie Buckingham
Melbourne, Florida

1
THINGS WILL BE DIFFERENT

Do you like to pray? Do you enjoy and look forward to prayer times, or do you find them boring and dry? Do you believe that things happen because you pray, or do you just go through the motions because you are supposed to? These are important questions we must ask if we are to take prayer seriously.

Prayer should be both enjoyable and effective if we expect to be devoted to prayer as the New Testament believers were. For that reason, I want to offer you some pointers on prayer and inspire you to pray more fervently and confidently. My purpose is to create a desire in you to reach out and touch the heart of God. I do not want merely to teach on prayer; I want to generate prayer. I am not interested in your learning about prayer; I am interested in *you praying*.

Let me begin by giving you three faith statements about prayer. When these statements are understood, they will inspire you to believe and will help prayer become a vital, enjoyable part of your Christian life.

1. *Things will be different because I pray.* If you pray for your son, your wife, or your husband, things will be different than they would have been. I mean that. Because I prayed for my son this morning, I believe his day will be different than it would have been. I prayed for India this morning, and I believe things will be different in India. Prayer has an effect; it is worthwhile.

2. *The throne of grace is wide open to me.* This is an important statement. The throne of grace is wide open to you, and anything *on God's heart* is available to you—if you pray. Prayer is centered around the throne of grace.

3. *Nothing is born without conception.* Natural conception doesn't just happen; there must be a physical union. Similarly, an answer to prayer doesn't just happen; there must be a union with God. Prayer is not a hit-or-miss proposition—today I hit, tomorrow I miss. God operates on the basis of principles found in Scripture. If we line up with God's heart and God's Scripture, our spirit is put in union with His Spirit, and conception takes place. Only when conception takes place is an answer to prayer born.

Do these statements inspire more faith in you? They inspire me and make me eager to pray because I know they are true.

Something Will Happen

A good place to begin our discussion of these faith statements is James 5:16: "The effectual fervent prayer of a righteous man availeth much" (*KJV*). To produce the full impact of this verse, I have developed a composite translation of my own: "The earnest, continual, heartfelt, fervent prayer of a godly man (or woman) releases mighty power and effects." The word "fervent" in the *King James Version* implies *continuation*. Therefore, I believe that the prayer of James 5:16 is earnest, continual, and heartfelt.

Notice the second part of the verse: the prayer of a godly person "releases mighty power and effects." Something will happen when a godly person begins and continues to pray with all his heart. When we pray, mighty effects are released. Prayer causes things to happen in your marriage, your church, or your pastor's sermon.

When you pray, "My God, speak to our pastor this Sunday. Anoint him, and flow through him. Give him a word of wisdom and a word of knowledge. Give him food for us, Father," your pastor will preach better. Things will be different on Sunday morning than they would have been because you, or you and your spouse, prayed a continual, heartfelt, fervent prayer. That prayer will release mighty miracles.

If you came to me with a problem, and I told you to pray about it, what would you think? You would probably think I had nothing to offer and simply put you off with a cliche—"pray about it."

Somehow, when we hear the word "prayer," we think "boredom" and "ineffectiveness." Why do you suppose that happens? It isn't God's fault. Satan tries to discourage us from realizing that the mighty power of prayer releases effects and miracles. This "Ho hum, he told me to pray" feeling is from the devil. The idea that prayer is a boring and ineffective task for times when nothing else can be said or done is completely false. James says that the effective, fervent prayer of a righteous man *avails*—it *accomplishes something!*

We are called to affect the destiny of our children, our marriages, our churches, and our nations. You can affect nations! Moscow is not going to rule this world. The Church is going to rule this world through intercession rather than domination.

Devotion To Prayer

Do you like to pray? I want prayer to be your greatest source of enjoyment. Although prayer is work, it can be your most delightful labor and your most important occupation.

Notice Colossians 4:12-13:

> Epaphras, who is one of you, a servant
> of Christ, greets you, always laboring
> fervently for you in prayers, that you

may stand perfect and complete in all the will of God. For I bear him witness that he has a great zeal for you, and those who are in Laodicea, and those in Hierapolis.

Have you ever heard of Epaphras? He is certainly not as well-known as Paul, Timothy, or Titus. Nevertheless, Epaphras is mentioned in Holy Scripture because he was an intercessor, and his chief delight was prayer. Paul mentions his zeal because Epaphras prayed continually that believers would stand "perfect and complete in all the will of God."

You may say, "Well, I'm just an unknown. I just go to church. I'm just the little old lady in the third row. I feel so inadequate." If you are an intercessor, you are one of the most important people in your pastor's congregation. Every pastor needs a whole crew praying for him, his wife, his family, the church, and the elder board. Every church needs several Epaphrases.

What a wonderful thing to have people devoted to prayer! Devotion to prayer is to be in love with it. The word "devoted" is found several times in the book of Acts, especially in the *New American Standard Bible*.

Acts 1:14 says,

These all with one mind were continually devoting themselves to prayer, along with the women, and Mary the mother of Jesus, and with His brothers—*NASB*.

They were devoted to prayer. This is the last mention of Mary, the mother of Jesus, in the Bible. And what was she doing? She was at a prayer meeting—*devoted* to prayer.

These people "prayed in" the first Pentecost. The Bible says that out of this prayer meeting there came "a sound . . . as of a rushing mighty wind, and it filled the whole house" (Acts 2:2). Tongues of fire came and sat on their heads, and "they were all filled with the Holy Spirit and began to speak with other tongues, as the Spirit gave them utterance" (Acts 2:4).

Do you know why we do not have more fullness in the Holy Spirit? We do not have people devoted to prayer. Do you think it is important that a prayer meeting established the first Pentecost? Talk about mighty effects and power! When we begin to pray, we prepare ourselves for an outpouring of the Holy Spirit.

Note also Acts 2:42:

And they were continually devoting themselves to the apostles' teaching and to fellowship, to the breaking of bread and to prayer—*NASB*.

This is immediately following the Pentecostal sermon. In fact, Acts 2:41 says that three thousand people were born again and baptized in water. This early Church established itself immediately in four areas. Its members devoted themselves to the apostles' doctrine (today's Scriptures), fellowship, the breaking of bread (either communion or eating house to house), and prayer. The early Church was based upon, among other things, a devotion to prayer. Prayer was a delight.

Commenting about the early Church's prayer life, this passage in Acts describes what happened during one of their meetings:

> And when they had been released, they went to their own companions, and reported all that the chief priests and the elders had said to them. And when they heard this, they lifted their voices to God with one accord. . . . And when they had prayed, the place where they had gathered together was shaken, and they were all filled with the Holy Spirit, and began to speak the word of God with boldness—Acts 4:23-24,31 *NASB*.

We often want the power of God without seeking Him. The Bible says that the place where the disciples were gathered together was shaken. They prayed with such power that they could actually feel the room shake. That was no earthquake—it was the power of God. The Bible says they were refilled. They had already been baptized with the Holy Spirit once, but now they were filled again.

Our problem is that we do not get on our faces before God to get refilled. We can only be baptized with the Holy Spirit once, but there can be many fillings. Prayer leads to being refilled. The Bible says that after these believers were refilled, they went out and spoke the Word of God with *boldness*. We will not have the power, the miracles, the boldness, or the souls saved unless we pray first.

The early Church was devoted to prayer, and every time they prayed the Spirit started moving. Their prayers were continual, heartfelt, fervent prayers that released mighty power and effects. Ours can be the same.

2

RELEASING THE POWER OF GRACE

In Paul's epistle to Titus, he tells us specifically what God's grace will do for us:

> For the grace of God that brings salvation has appeared to all men, teaching us that, denying ungodliness and worldly lusts, we should live soberly, righteously, and godly in the present age, looking for the blessed hope and glorious appearing of our great God and Savior Jesus Christ, who gave Himself for us, that He might redeem us from every lawless deed and purify for Himself His own special people, zealous for good works. Speak these things, exhort, and rebuke with all authority. Let no one despise you—Titus 2:11-15.

This passage concerns holiness. God never gives us grace as a license to sin. He gives us grace to get out of sin, to have victory, to forgive, to be kind, to have a pure and holy mind, to have right motives, and to be a man or woman of integrity. Thus, when we speak about grace and prayer, we are not speaking about forgiveness that allows us to continue sinning. We are speaking of the grace of God that brings salvation and deliverance.

Grace teaches us to "deny ungodliness and worldly lust." When? When we die? No! It says we should "live soberly, righteously, and godly *in the present age.*" That's exciting! The Bible even says that Jesus "gave Himself for us [that's grace—Calvary!], that He might redeem us from every lawless deed and purify for Himself His own special people, zealous [excited and enthusiastic] for good works"—a people excited about not having to live in sin; excited about abiding in Christ; and excited about walking in the light.

When I talk about grace and prayer, I am talking about *victory.* I am talking about praying through the problems in your life until they cease to exist.

This scripture says that we do not have to sin. Have you ever heard a preacher say, "Everyone sins every day in thought, word, and deed"? I don't think that is true. I don't sin every day in thought, word, and deed, and you don't have to either. If you can have victory for five minutes, then you can have it for an hour. If you can have it for an hour, then you can have it for a day.

18

The grace of God has appeared, teaching us to deny ungodliness and worldly lust. We can live sensibly and righteously. I am talking about prayer and grace—grace to be pure, holy, sensible, and righteous. We can be different, redeemed from every lawless deed.

If you are a sincere Christian, you do not only want forgiveness—you want cleansing. 1 John 1:9 says, "If we confess our sins, He is faithful and just to forgive us our sins, and to cleanse us from all unrighteousness."

"Forgiveness" means not having to go to hell. But "cleansing" means a spring cleaning of your heart.

What would you say if someone came forward in your church and said, "I want to be forgiven, but please don't cleanse me because I am planning to commit the same sin tonight"? You would say he was a hypocrite. In the same way, the Lord wants to forgive *and* cleanse you. The grace of God brings salvation and deliverance, teaching us to deny "ungodliness and worldly lusts" and "to live soberly, righteously, and godly." He purifies us to Himself as a special people "zealous of good works." I don't know if that excites you, but it should.

The Danger Of Bitter Roots

In another verse about grace, we are exhorted to be "looking diligently lest anyone fall short of the grace of God; lest any root of bitterness springing up cause trouble, and by this many become defiled" (Hebrews 12:15).

Look at the verse again. It says to look *diligently.* Why? You must make sure that no one falls short of the grace of God, for this can lead to developing a root of bitterness. And what does a root of bitterness do? It "causes trouble and defiles many."

Preachers preach about many sins: don't smoke, don't drink, don't curse, don't commit adultery, etc. But the sin that most Christians have is a root of bitterness. Hate, anger, and poison spring up and come out of the mouth. And the Bible says that "many are defiled."

You must understand that slandering, gossiping, whispering, backbiting, griping, complaining, grumbling, and murmuring are only surface sins that come out of a root of bitterness. When somebody complains or gossips, his problem is not the murmuring and the complaining—his problem is *unresolved bitterness* in his heart. Because that hate is there, venom pours out when he opens his mouth.

Have you ever known anyone who took up someone else's offense? Psalm 15:13 says to not take up another's offense because you pick up the root of bitterness that has caused him to bad-mouth, backbite, complain, and accuse. Because he is your friend, you are also offended; and the scripture comes true—a root of bitterness springs up, and many people become defiled.

Why does this happen? It happens because someone is not "looking diligently, lest anyone fall short of the grace of God." God gives us grace to forgive, but that grace moves from theory into our heart *by prayer.*

I remember kneeling with my wife, so hurt that all I could pray was, "I don't want to forgive. I want to stay mad. I want to stay hurt."

While we were out of town preaching at a revival meeting, one of the chief elders of our church moved the pulpit down on the floor. He said that he was preaching the truth, commanded everybody to be rebaptized in water, and stated that the only reason the pulpit had been on the platform was that ours was an elevated ministry. The whole church was divided, and he attempted to take over.

My attitude was, "They can take that church and run with it. Phooey on the whole bunch of them. I don't want to pastor. I want out of this." Those were the first roots of bitterness going down. I knelt and said, "I don't want to change, but I know that the spirit I am in is not the Holy Spirit. And I ask for You to change me, even though I do not want to change." I availed myself of the grace of God.

Scripture says that we must be "looking diligently lest anyone fall short of the grace of God." The grace is there, but you must *avail yourself of that grace* by getting down on your knees and saying, "Jesus, I don't have any love left; give me Your love. Please wash my anger away with Your blood. Give me love again."

Then ask the Lord to heal your wounded spirit. Avail yourself of grace. "Lord Jesus, heal my wounded spirit. I don't care, and I don't want to care. And I don't care that I don't care!" That is the way I felt that day. You have to be honest when you pray. After all, God knows how you feel.

There we knelt—a broken, wounded young pastor and his wife. Our prayer was, "You said You would heal the brokenhearted. Heal my broken heart. You said that You would free those who are bruised, and I am bruised. Heal my bruises, and give me love for those people. I choose to forgive them even though they don't deserve it because You forgave me when I didn't deserve it."

You may expect me to say that lightning hit me and I immediately felt bubbly. I didn't feel anything. But when I got up off my knees, I knew that I had turned everything over to Jesus.

Recovering from a wounded spirit is like recovering from surgery; it is not always instantaneous. First you must learn how to walk again. Then you begin to regain your strength. Then the soreness begins to leave the wound. The scar is still there, but it begins to fade. Finally, after a period of time, the scar is hardly noticeable. The procedure is the same with a wound in the spirit.

I healed more quickly than my wife. I believe that when women get wounded, because they are more sensitive and more emotional (and that's a good quality), they are hurt more deeply. My wife testified that for six months she worshipped God in our church but did not feel a thing—not even the presence of the Holy Spirit. She worshipped out of obedience and lifted her hands because she knew that the Scripture instructed her to do so. But eventually the joy began to come back, and she regained the peace and satisfaction of being in the ministry.

What did we do? Instead of letting a root of bitterness eat away and defile many, we asked God to give us love and heal our wounded spirit. We relinquished all right to judge others. This prayer worked. That was almost fifteen years ago, and we are still in the ministry, happily pastoring the same church—*Full Faith Church of Love.* But how many ministers have left broken and are now selling insurance or doing other things because of a wounded, bitter spirit?

I do not want to leave this verse too quickly because it is very serious. Read it again. Bitterness will not only cause trouble for you (although that would be bad enough), but it will trouble your children. Sitting around the supper table and tearing down a church and its leaders will defile your whole family. You will defile your daughters. You will defile your home group. You will defile *everyone* who touches you. Your bitterness will be a contagious and infectious cancer to everyone you know.

To have bitterness in your heart is wicked, not only because it is personal sin that is not forsaken but because it destroys many other people. I personally know of whole churches that have been ruined by a root of bitterness. I know entire families that have been destroyed by a root of bitterness. I know what bitterness can do.

God's Mountain Movers

People fall short of the grace of God by retaining bitterness instead of praying for Jesus to take it away. How do you receive the grace of God? By getting down on your knees and praying. Put yourself underneath Jesus' blood and avail yourself of God's love, God's grace, and God's forgiveness.

Look at Zechariah 4:6-7:

> So he answered and said to me: "This is the word of the Lord to Zerubbabel: 'Not by might nor by power, but by My Spirit,' says the Lord of hosts. 'Who are you, O great mountain. Before Zerubbabel you shall become a plain! And he shall bring forth the capstone with shouts of "Grace, grace to it." ' "

Zerubbabel faced a mountain, and God said simply, "Not by might nor by power, but by My Spirit." Most of us are familiar with this verse.

But verse seven is also for us. Here God tells Zerubbabel to shout to the mountain, "Grace, grace."

Are you aware that the Lord Jesus Christ calls us to be mountain movers? (See Mark 11:23.) He tells us that we must speak to them. It is not enough simply to talk about the mountains. We must say, "Be removed!"

Have you ever had a mountain move in your life—a mountain of depression, fear, unclean thoughts, anger, bad habits, etc.? You must shout "Grace!" to that mountain. You have to say, "I put the grace of God right in your face; and you, great mountain, you *will* become a plain!"

That great mountain in your life can be knocked flat by the grace of God. Instead of letting it sit on top of you, speak to it. "Alcoholism—lust—anger—I command you by the grace and name of Jesus to loose me." That mountain will lie down.

The key to prayer is that *God is on your side!* The key to that alliance is grace, which simply means God's enablement—God's power and ability released. You can overcome any sin and any mountain by the grace of God. But you must speak to it again and again, until you can say, "It wasn't by my might or my power; it was by the Spirit of the Lord. As I shouted, 'Grace!' the mountain moved."

3

GOD'S OPEN THRONE
OF GRACE

In the first chapter, we considered the faith statement that things will be different because we pray. The second faith statement forms the basis for the first. Your prayers are effective because *the throne of grace is wide open to you.* Anything that is on God's heart is available to you if you pray.

This statement is best illustrated in one of the most exciting verses on prayer in the entire Bible:

> Let us therefore come boldly to the throne of grace, that we may obtain mercy and find grace to help in time of need—Hebrews 4:16.

First of all, notice that the verse says to "come boldly." You do not have to come like a whipped pup. You do not have to come saying, "I'm so unworthy." Of course you're unworthy. Everyone is unworthy without the precious blood of Jesus washing him clean of all sin. Nevertheless, the

Bible says to "come boldly" and with confidence. Why? Because the blood of Jesus has made you worthy to approach God.

March right up to God, knowing that the One who sits on the throne died for you and loves you. The Lord Jesus loves you and strongly desires to help you. God is not an unwilling God who has to be coerced into helping you. He is more willing to help you than you are to ask for help.

God's throne is not a throne of judgment. Neither the word "judgment" nor the word "accusation" is written across His throne. The devil is the accusor of the brethren. Written upon God's throne is the word *GRACE*.

What tremendous peace and assurance flood my heart when I come to God and He says, "Come, and come boldly." He invites us to a throne of grace and says that we may obtain mercy.

The word "mercy" implies that we have sinned and are not perfect. One only needs mercy because he has failed or is less than he could be. At God's throne we will find mercy and grace to help in time of need.

Do you have a need—financial, marital, emotional, mental, etc.? Do you need victory in your thought life or over a certain habit? What is your need? God says to come boldly to the throne of grace that you may find His grace and power. *Grace is God's ability and God's enablement,* and you can find it in your time of need.

The devil says that you may as well not come. You have blown it and have too many needs—it is hopeless for you to pray. Those concepts are exactly opposed to Scripture.

Let us consider another passage concerning grace:

> Therefore the Lord longs to be gracious to you, and therefore He waits on high to have compassion on you. For the Lord is a God of justice; how blessed are all those who long for Him—Isaiah 30:18 *NASB*.

The Bible says the Lord "longs" to be gracious to you. He is *eager* to be gracious. He waits on high to have compassion on *you*. In fact, I want you to personalize this verse: "The Lord is longing to be gracious to *me*, and He is waiting on high to show *me* compassion." No matter what the devil says, the throne of grace is wide open to you.

God's Gracious Heart

If I were the devil and I read Hebrews 4:16 and Isaiah 30:18, I would do everything I could to keep Christians from praying. Do you ever wonder why you talk about prayer, you teach about prayer, you hear sermons on prayer, but you don't pray? Satan fights your praying because he knows that God longs to answer your prayers with compassion and grace. He knows that your prayers will affect you and your circumstances.

Have you ever prayed and suddenly found your whole temperament changed? Once I felt so discouraged that I was ready to leave the ministry. Then I stopped and prayed with a friend. Instantaneously, the spirit of depression lifted from me, and I began to smile. I was shocked that it worked! It surprised me that my attitude could change so abruptly and quickly. What was the difference? I prayed.

You need to pray for your children, not just have teaching about prayer. Pray for your children, your spouse, your finances, and your decisions. Isaiah tells us that the Lord "longs" to be gracious to us and waits on high to have compassion on us. The Bible paints a picture of a God eager for someone to bring their problems to Him.

Isaiah 33:2 says much the same thing:

> O Lord, be gracious to us; we have waited for Thee. Be Thou their strength every morning, salvation also in the time of distress—*NASB*.

This is talking about an appointment with God. When you wait on God every morning, He will be your salvation.

Notice that the Bible says "in the time of distress." The devil will try to convince you that you are too wicked or too far away from God to pray. But God says otherwise.

In the middle of the night, not long ago, the Lord spoke to me concerning His grace. He said that on Sunday morning I should tell the divorced people in my congregation, "The Lord says, 'I will touch you.'" He said, "I want you to tell them they are not untouchable, and they are not lepers."

You may be a divorcee who feels far from God. It does not make any difference even if you were the guilty party. Even if you were 95 percent responsible for the divorce, God says, "I am longing to be gracious." Men and preachers may judge and condemn, but God says, "I will touch you."

You may be crushed because you have had an abortion. But the good news is that the Lord is longing to be gracious to you. He is waiting to help you. You can say, "I am not a leper. God will touch me. Maybe some self-righteous church member won't, but my God will."

Breaking Old Bondages

Sometimes we *feel* like lepers. Do you remember the story of the leper who came to Jesus and said, "If you will, you can make me clean"? Jesus said to him, "I will, be thou made clean." (See Mark 1:40-41.) The Bible says that Jesus touched him.

Jesus will touch you, too. You are not untouchable. You are never too old, too busy, or too sinful—you are never too anything to change. You can change, and prayer makes the difference. All things *are* possible with God. You *can* make a fresh start.

How do you make this new beginning? You must begin to pray. The throne of grace is wide open to you, and anything on God's heart is available to you. You can improve. Through prayer, you can become a better person. Prayer is dependence upon God.

You say, "But I've prayed again and again and again." Well, keep praying. But begin by asking God why your prayer is not being answered. Ask Him where you are not matching up with the Holy Spirit. He said that He is *waiting* on high to show us love and give us victory. The lack of victory is not due to God's reluctance.

For example, a believer had prayed for years about smoking but had not overcome it. While it may be a little thing to some, to him it was important. And as he prayed and asked God to reveal what was blocking the victory, God showed him the real problem.

This man found that he had started smoking out of rebellion to his parents. What needed to be dealt with was rebellion, not smoking. God revealed that rebellion and helped the man eliminate it. He became different and did quit smoking.

On a flight home recently, I sat next to a sixteen-year-old young lady. Because she was young and I did not want to come on like gangbusters, I just sat and read my Bible for about half the flight. Finally, I turned to talk to her a moment and asked her a little bit about her relationship with the Lord. She was a Baptist and had met the Lord when she was eleven. I told her that I got saved in a Baptist church at age nine.

Then the Spirit of God began to stir around inside me, and I received a prophecy for her. I knew she would not understand a prophecy, so I wrote it across my business card and handed it to her. The word of the Lord was, "You can become twice as much as you can imagine."

I believe that word is for all of us: *You can become twice as much as you imagine.* You and I have much more potential than we realize. Experts tell us that we only use 20 percent of the capacity of our brains—let's broaden that concept to our spiritual gifts, our smiles, our encouragement, and our love.

The Heart Of Prayer

The little word of encouragement I gave to that teenager will stick with her because it was prophecy. But now I want you to think about what I told her—you can become twice as much as you can imagine. The root of "imagine" is "image." Develop an image of yourself. Whatever you can imagine about yourself is only half of what you can become.

You can change. That is the whole point of prayer. That is the whole point of the Bible. If you can't change—if you have to be the way you are—shut the Bible! Pitch it! Why should I preach if you can't grow? There is no need for church if you can't grow.

But you *can* grow, and growth means change. At the center of all change is prayer. And at the center of prayer is God's open throne of grace. He is waiting to be gracious to you, and anything on His heart is available to you if you will pray.

Look now at 2 Corinthians 12:9-10. Read this passage out loud until it sinks deeply into your spirit:

> And He said to me, "My grace is sufficient for you, for My strength is made perfect in weakness." Therefore most gladly I will rather boast in my infirmities, that the power of Christ may rest upon me. Therefore I take pleasure in infirmities, in reproaches, in needs, in persecutions, in distresses, for Christ's sake. For when I am weak, then I am strong.

Not only is God's grace *available* to you, but it is *sufficient* for you. Notice that the word "my" refers to God twice. Paul says that *God's* grace—not your grace—is sufficient for you. In fact, God's strength is made perfect in weakness. Have you ever considered the fact that your strength is your weakness, and your weakness is your strength?

As a young pastor, I remember telling the chairman of our deacon board about a pastor I knew in the city. This pastor had just taken authority over a situation in his church and had ramrodded through what needed to be done. I said, "Boy, I wish I were strong like that."

This dear man of God said, "But Ernie, that's why we love you so much. You're *not* like that. You *don't* ramrod. You *don't* dictate." What I had conceived of as a weakness was really a strength.

God's strength is made perfect in our weakness. Be encouraged to talk to God, remembering that "the throne of grace is wide open to you." In all of our weakness, God is able to become strong in us and make us tools for His purposes.

One of the most important things that makes you a tool of God, filled with the power of God, is prayer. Prayer takes us to the throne of grace, where we find help in time of need.

4

SPIRITUAL UNION WITH GOD

The third faith statement I have given you concerning prayer is that *nothing is born without conception*. In other words, conception does not just happen—union with God is required. In the natural realm, conception leading to birth cannot happen without a physical union; and in the spiritual realm, conception of a spiritual reality leading to its manifestation cannot happen without a spiritual union with God.

While driving to church one Sunday morning, I was meditating on the subject of prayer. Praying in the Spirit, I heard the Lord speak to me clearly. He said, "Nothing is birthed without intercession." The Lord said seriously, "That person whose salvation you are praying for will go to hell unless somebody touches God for him. The marriage you are concerned about will end in divorce unless somebody touches God. That alcoholic or drug addict will not become free unless somebody touches God."

I began to understand that nothing is born in another person except by intercession. Intercession is required for conception to take place.

If this principle is true, then every one of us must seriously consider *what* he is praying and whether he needs to *change his whole life* to include prayer and intercession. I do not believe anyone can get saved unless someone intercedes. I do not believe any marriage can be a good marriage without intercession. I do not believe healing can occur without intercession. *Anything* that requires a move of God requires intercession.

Isaiah 66:7 says, "Before she travailed, she gave birth; before her pain came, she delivered a male child." Notice that *before she travailed*—that is before Zion or the believers travailed—*she gave birth*. And what was born? "A male child." That is a prophecy concerning the Lord Jesus Christ.

"Who has heard such a thing? who has seen such things?" (Isaiah 66:8). Who has heard of such a thing as God becoming a man? Who has seen such a thing as a virgin birth? Who has seen God manifested in the flesh?

Verse 8 goes on to prophesy about a time prior to the Second Coming. "Shall the earth be made to give birth in one day? or shall a nation be born at once?" This passage refers to the 1948 birth of Israel.

Following this birth of the nation of Israel, the passage concerns the next stage of the prophetic time clock—a time of intercession. " 'For as soon as Zion travailed, she gave birth to her children. Shall I bring to the time of birth, and not cause delivery?' says the Lord. 'Shall I who cause delivery shut up the womb?' says your God'' (Isaiah 66:8-9).

This time between the birth of Israel and the coming of the Lord is when Zion is to travail and give birth. *This,* then, is the day of travail—the time of intercession. Nothing is born in this day without genuine union with God in our spirits.

A Touch Of Faith

I hope this stimulates you to say, "My God, I haven't been praying. Forgive me for my sin of prayerlessness."

I hope you realize that the curse on your marriage, your life, or your walk with God is that you have not been praying. Things are going to get worse—not better—with prayerlessness. If anything is to change, you must touch God.

This principle is best illustrated in the story of the woman who had a flow of blood for twelve years:

> When she heard about Jesus, she came behind Him in the crowd and touched His garment; for she said, "If only I may touch His clothes, I shall be made well." Immediately the fountain of her blood was dried up, and she felt in her body

> that she was healed of the affliction. And
> Jesus, immediately knowing in Himself
> that power had gone out of Him, turned
> around in the crowd and said, "Who
> touched My clothes?"—Mark 5:27-30.

Many people were in that crowd, yet Jesus noticed that one particular person touched Him. This woman touched Him with a touch of faith. Many people bumped into Jesus. In fact, when He said, "Who touched Me?" the disciples did not understand. "What do you mean who touched You? They're *all* bumping into You."

But there is a difference between bumping into Jesus and touching Him. Although an entire congregation worships and sings, often only a few people actually touch Jesus. The rest mouth the words and are possibly even sincere; but the Spirit does not come upon them. Only the person who loses himself in God touches Him. And when He is touched, Jesus in heaven turns to the Father and says, "I felt power go out from Me."

That is what the old Pentecostals meant when they said, "Pray until you've prayed." They did not mean praying through your unbelief. They meant praying until you knew you had an answer.

This woman said, "If I can just touch Him." That should be our heart's cry. When we touch Him, power will come forth from Jesus into us. We have to travail—we have to pray until we know we have touched Him and something is born.

For conception to occur, union is required. Babies don't just happen. We may joke, "Well, they drink out of that water fountain. . . ." But how many babies have been born because someone drank out of a water fountain? I am being silly, but I hope to make a point.

When a believer's spirit touches the Spirit of God, and when his will and God's will meet, union takes place. Out of that union comes a birthing: someone is saved, a marriage is restored, someone gets a new job, etc. These prayer answers come because this person did more than rub elbows with God, sing songs, have an appointment with God, or read his Bible. Somehow, his spirit got in union with the Spirit of God. When that happens, something good will result.

Isaiah talks about this concept in chapter 66 when he says, "As soon as Zion travailed. . . ." Sometimes we hope that birthing just happens. It does not "just happen" in the spiritual realm any more than in the natural realm. No, when something is born it is because someone had so much love that they sneaked through the crowd—sneaked through the religion and the rigamarole—and touched Him.

Mark 6:56 tells us that "as many as touched Him were made whole." That principle is still true today—as many as are put in union with Jesus by touching the Spirit of God will be made whole.

41

Praying The Word

This concept of travailing until birthing takes
place is further illustrated in 1 Kings 18:41-46.

> Elijah said to Ahab, "Go up, eat and
> drink; for there is the sound of abun-
> dance of rain." So Ahab went up to eat
> and drink. And Elijah went up to the top
> of Carmel; then bowed down on the
> ground, and put his face between his
> knees, and said to his servant, "Go up
> now, look toward the sea." So he went
> up and looked, and said, "There is noth-
> ing." And seven times he said, *"Go
> again."* Then it came to pass the seventh
> time, that he said, "There is a cloud, as
> small as a man's hand, rising out of the
> sea!" So he said, "Go up, say to Ahab,
> 'Prepare your chariot and go down
> before the rain stops you.' " Now it
> happened in the meantime that the sky
> became black with clouds and wind,
> and there was a heavy rain—*Italics
> added*.

Elijah prophesied that there would be the
"sound of abundance of rain," but he did more
than prophesy. He bowed down on the ground and
put his face between his knees, similar to the tradi-
tional Middle East birthing position. At first, there

was no response to his prayer. He sent his servant to look at the sky. The servant came back six times, and each time the answer was, "There is nothing." This is often true of what we say about our prayer.

Although he prophesied an abundance of rain, he did not seem to think the prophecy was enough. *He prayed the prophecy.* He was trying to birth it. He knew the Word of the Lord, and he prayed it. Finally, the seventh time there appeared "a cloud the size of a hand." He then told his servant to tell Ahab to get down before his chariot got stuck in the mud.

James 5:17-18 tells us that "Elijah was a man with a nature like ours." He was no super saint, he was just like us. Yet, "he prayed earnestly that it would not rain; and it did not rain on the land for three years and six months."

Notice the next phrase: *"And he prayed again."* Would you say that aloud? How many times did he pray again? We know from the Old Testament that he prayed seven times. "And the heaven gave rain, and the earth produced its fruit."

You say, "Well, I've already prayed." Pray again and again and again. Pray until you have touched God, and your prayer receives an answer. You must pray until you have the witness of the Holy Spirit that victory is on the way. Look for rain. Elijah would not stop praying until he saw that cloud.

Elijah combined prophecy with prayer. Prophecy is not enough, and prayer is not enough. The formula was *Prophecy + Prayer = Rain.*

For us, the Word of God plus intercession equals restoration. Scripture is not enough. There must be prayer. We have to pray that scripture. On the other hand, intercession is not enough. There must be scripture.

The key to effective praying is to gain a revelation from the Bible that fits your circumstance. Once you have the Word of the Lord, you are half done. Then, after praying that scripture, birthing takes place and restoration occurs.

This is one of the most important principles concerning prayer. It requires two things to bring a revival, a miracle, salvation, a restoration of marriage, or an answer to prayer.

Did the prophet say, "I have the Word of God, and I have the will of God. God has spoken to me, and I have prophesied. Therefore my responsibility is done"? A thousand times, no! Elijah, having the will of God, began to pray it. *When Scripture is combined with intercession, birthing takes place.* Unless there is both the Word of God and intercession, there won't be *any* answer to prayer.

Nothing is birthed without *travail*—hard-fought intercession. Babies must be pushed out. Birth requires birth pangs. Nor does conception just happen. There must be a union.

How do you know that you have touched God? When your spirit is put into union with the Spirit and will of God, you will experience such peace and joy that you will know you have touched Him. Then birthing will come to pass.

Scriptures For Prayer

I would like to end this chapter by suggesting some prayers that you can begin praying now. We do not need to learn more about prayer, we need to begin praying. Therefore, here are some scriptures that you can begin combining with intercession right now. But remember, these scriptures are no good to you without your travailing in prayer. You can pray these for your grandchildren, your children, or for somebody else's children.

1. *Isaiah 44:3-5:*

> " 'For I will pour water on him who is thirsty, and floods on the dry ground; I will pour My Spirit on your descendants, and My blessing on your offspring; they will spring up among the grass like willows by the watercourses.' One will say, 'I am the Lord's'; another will call himself by the name of Jacob; another will write on his hand, 'The Lord's,' and name himself by the name of Israel."

2. *Isaiah 54:13:*

> "All your children shall be taught by the Lord, and great shall be the peace of your children."

3. *Isaiah 59:21:*

"As for Me," says the Lord, "this is My covenant with them: My Spirit who is upon you, and My words which I have put in your mouth, shall not depart from your mouth, nor from the mouth of your descendants, nor from the mouth of your descendants' descendants . . . from this time and forever more."

4. *Jeremiah 31:15-16:*

Thus says the Lord: "A voice was heard in Ramah, lamentation and bitter weeping, Rachel weeping for her children, refusing to be comforted for her children, because they are no more . . . Refrain your voice from weeping, and your eyes from tears; for your works shall be rewarded, says the Lord, and they shall come back from the land of the enemy."

Begin to pray these scriptures for your children and grandchildren. Pray until you have touched God as Elijah did, until you see His Word come to pass in the lives of your children. Pray also for your parents, your spouse, and your friends. Don't stop praying until you see a rain cloud on the horizon—until you see God's answer.

5

LEARNING TO LEAN ON GOD

One serious problem many people have in regard to prayer is trusting someone other than God. In this chapter, I will provide you with a scriptural understanding of the provision Jesus has made for us through His resurrection and ascension.

Let us begin by considering Hebrews 7:25:

> Therefore He is also able to save to the uttermost those who come to God through Him, since He ever lives to make intercession for them.

Notice that phrase, "Those who come to God *through Him.*" He will not save to the uttermost those who come to Him through a saint, Mary, a pastor, an apostle, or any other person. He will save those who come to God "through Him."

Do not fool yourself; this is not an attack on

Catholics. This "Hail Mary Syndrome" in our approach to God is as much Protestant as anything else.

Jesus is a High Priest (can we say Prayer Warrior?) and is fighting for us. He is holy, harmless, undefiled, and separate from sinners. He has become higher than the heavens and does not need to offer up sacrifices daily. We already have a High Priest, who "ever lives," not merely to sit on the throne of God but "to make intercession" for us. (See Hebrews 7:26-27.)

Do you believe these verses? Do you believe that Jesus lives to make intercession for you? Do you believe that you don't need anyone else to serve as your High Priest? Many of us never see Jesus as a High Priest. We see Him portrayed as Savior and Lord, but we seldom see Him portrayed as High Priest. An understanding of all three is essential to a healthy Christian walk.

Jesus—Savior And Lord

The first important aspect to consider is Jesus' ministry as Savior. We need a revelation of this ministry to gain an inward assurance of forgiveness and justification. Although I was saved when I was nine years old, I did not have the assurance of my salvation until I was nineteen. People who are saved as children often have a greater struggle gaining assurance of their salvation than those whose lives undergo a dramatic transformation. In any case, I began to doubt my salvation.

One day, however, I became convinced that if my salvation depended even one percent on me, I was going to go to hell. Realizing that my faith had to be in either Jesus' blood or my works, I realized that my only hope of escaping hell was the blood of Jesus. 1 John 1:7 became an anchor to me:

> But if we walk in the light as He is in the light, we have fellowship with one another, and the blood of Jesus Christ His Son cleanses us from all sin.

When I began to put my faith in the blood of Jesus and to understand that Jesus was my Savior, I obtained the assurance of my salvation.

An assurance of salvation is different from salvation itself. Nevertheless, it is essential to a healthy, peaceful life in God. That assurance can only come from resting wholeheartedly on one thing—the blood of Jesus Christ.

The second important aspect of Jesus' ministry is His position as resurrected Lord. Upon gaining a revelation of the resurrection of the Lord and seeing that He not only died for us but also rose for us and lives within us, we gain victory and sanctification. It is a wonderful thing when we really believe that He is in us, not in theory but in reality. If you can become conscious of the fact that the power of the Godhead is inside of you, you will conquer lust. You will conquer hate. You will conquer *anything!*

Paul saw this reality and stated in Galatians 2:20:

> I am crucified with Christ: nevertheless I live; yet not I, but Christ liveth in me: and the life which I now live in the flesh I live by the faith of the Son of God, who loved me, and gave himself for me—*KJV*.

When you see what Paul saw, you will also begin to see your potential.

The best way I can explain this sense of the resurrection is with a story about a lady in Arkansas who had been in a mental institution twice. She was constantly depressed and defeated, was thoroughly discouraged, and hated herself. I was conducting a seminar nearby. The second night she came up to me and said, "I see it."

I said, "What do you see?"

She said, "All my life I've been trying to get Jesus inside me. Now I see that He *is* in me, and I have to let Him out."

He is in you, and He is never going to get "in" any more than He is already. The issue is whether you are going to let Him out. You can get up every morning and say, "I am a river of love, joy, peace, gentleness, patience, goodness, and meekness. I am going to let Jesus out of me."

You will finally see your potential. Knowing your potential in God is different than knowing you are forgiven. But to walk in both peace and victory, you must grasp both the forgiveness found in Jesus as Savior and the potential found in Jesus as Lord. When you grasp both of these realities, you will be two-thirds of the way toward a full, healthy walk.

The Master Intercessor

The third important aspect of victorious Christian living is gaining an understanding of Jesus' exaltation. When Jesus went back to heaven, His ministry did not end. He is alive, right now, praying for you. The key to prayer is to find out how the High Priest is praying; whenever you pray in agreement with Him, you will receive an answer.

Who are you agreeing with? Jesus—a High Priest who "is able to save to the uttermost those who come to God through Him, since He ever lives to make intercession for them." He is going to save us to the uttermost because He is exalted and sits at the right hand of God and prays for us.

Every week somebody drops a list of twenty-five prayer requests in the offering box, with eight requests for healing, ten requests for salvation, and every other kind of need. The person will literally take the time to write four or five pages of prayer requests and then say, "Brother Ernie, will you pray for these people?"

What are we saying when we ask that question? First, we are saying, "I know *my* prayers won't be answered." Second, we are saying, "I need to get someone to pray for me who I know can get his prayers answered." Third, we are saying, "I know I am not right with God, and I am not willing to repent to get right with God. And since I have no plans of repenting, I am looking desperately for a mediator. If it isn't Ernie Gruen, maybe Oral Roberts, T.L. Osborne, or Kenneth Copeland will do."

All of these statements indicate a lack of revelation and understanding that the Son of God Himself, who "is holy, harmless, undefiled, separate from sinners, and . . . higher than the heavens," is sitting on the throne saying, "I want to save you to the uttermost. I live to make intercession."

"Never mind, Jesus. I am going to Pastor So-and-so." Isn't that a ridiculous statement? Many of us go to our leaders and say, "Hail Pastor, full of grace, pray for me now in the hour of my need." When we approach a pastor, a home group leader, or any other person and say, in essence, "Hail Jim, Hail Jane, or Hail Sally—pray for me in the hour of my need," we are doing what many of our Catholic brothers and sisters do with the saints and Mary. We are placing our faith in someone other than the High Priest.

Why should we go to a man when we can go to God? Most do so because this third aspect of Jesus' ministry is not real to them. We have seen

Him as Savior and Lord, but many of us have never seen Him as the High Priest sitting in heaven waiting for us to talk to Him. He is waiting right now.

You say, "Man, I wish I could find somebody holy to pray for me." Hail Jesus! He is *holy.* "I wish I could find somebody undefiled." Hail Jesus! He is *undefiled.* "I wish I could find someone higher than the heavens." Hail Jesus! He is *higher than the heavens.* "For such a High Priest was fitting for us, who is *holy, harmless, undefiled, separate from sinners, and has become higher than the heavens;* who does not need daily, as those high priests, to offer sacrifices . . . for His own sins" (Hebrews 7:26-27, *Italics added*).

Nobody sitting in any sanctuary in the world can possibly match that list. Why do we look for another person? Because preachers preach on Christ's blood and His resurrection but do not preach on the exaltation, ascension, and High Priesthood of Jesus. And since these are seldom preached, we fail to see how able and eager Jesus is to hear and answer our prayers.

We need to be reminded of the High Priest's function. The High Priest of Scripture represents others to God. Jesus did not go back to heaven to sit down lazily and say, "You're on your own, folks." Remember the old theory that God wound up the world like a clock and let it tick on its own? Is that what Jesus did when he went back to heaven? Did He say, "Now, I died for you, rose for you, and indwelled you. Good luck, I hope

53

you make it''? No! The Bible says that Jesus is able to save to the uttermost those who come to God through Him since He ever lives to make intercession for them.

Therefore, it is a sin to make any person other than Jesus a mediator. Say that aloud. This is as much a Protestant problem as it is a Catholic problem.

> For there is one God and one Mediator between God and men, the Man Christ Jesus—1 Timothy 2:5.

How many mediators are there? One! When we run with a list of twenty prayer requests to any man, we are asking that man to be our high priest. Would you ask a pastor to be your savior or your lord? Then why ask a pastor to be your high priest? If you can get in your spirit a sense of Jesus' High Priesthood, your prayer life will be transformed.

Two-Way Healing

If the High Priest lives to make intercession, and if He is the Mediator, then the key to prayer is for you and your one Mediator to talk about your situation. If you can find out what the Lord Jesus is saying instead of what you are saying, then you will get God's answer and God's perspective. He is higher than the heavens. You will be talking to Number One.

Effective prayer involves more listening than talking. Prayer requires you to become a listener. You may think the solution to your problem is discipline. God may say, "Lay on the love." You may say, "Lay on some discipline." If a situation needs discipline and you give it love, or it needs love and you give it discipline, you can bring death. You must have a daily, up-to-date relationship with Jesus that consists of both talking and listening. If you are not hearing from God, you are in big trouble and will have to depend on man for advice.

Such a situation reminds me of King Saul. Unable to hear from God anymore, he went to a witch! If God does not talk to you, it will do you no good to go anywhere else. If God is not talking to you, it's your move. Get on your knees, and pray until the Spirit of God speaks to you. It is a sin to make any person other than Jesus a mediator. Can you say "Amen" to that sentence?

I call this whole problem of failing to go directly to Jesus "transferal," which is removing the responsibility from one person and placing it upon another person. This problem of prayer, this "Hail Mary Syndrome," is simply *transferal*. It is saying, "I am going to remove from myself the responsibility to pray for that person and place it onto that home group leader. I am going to remove—transfer—my responsibility to touch God." Ultimately, we are attempting to find someone other than Christ to be a mediator. But the Bible says that there is only *one* Mediator—Jesus.

Let us consider the logistics of transferring our responsibilities to a pastor. No human being can pray and touch God for hundreds of people. It is usually impossible for anyone to pray for your loved ones as well as you can. You know them. You love them. The heart, the love, and the compassion will be in *your* prayer.

No one else can get as stirred up about praying for my children as my wife, Dee, and I can. Someone else may give 60 or even 80 percent of their efforts in prayer for my children. But no one is likely to give one hundred percent except their mother and I. Praying for our children is our primary responsibility. Let us no longer come into prayer meetings to transfer our own responsibilities.

Now, there is a balance to this concept. Sometimes God will lead us to ask someone else to agree with us in prayer. But He will never lead us to transfer our own responsibility to pray to another person because He has provided a High Priest for each of us.

The Compassionate Priest

Ten times in the book of Hebrews we see Jesus as High Priest. You will never understand intercession until you understand the High Priesthood of Jesus. If you want to move into a deeper prayer life, you *must* understand these verses:

> Therefore, in all things He had to be made like His brethren, that He might be a merciful and faithful High Priest in things pertaining to God, to make propitiation for the sins of the people. For in that He Himself has suffered, being tempted, He is able to aid those who are tempted—Hebrews 2:17-18.

The Greek reads, "He is able *to run to* the aid of, run to the help of, those who are tempted."

This verse tells us that, as a human being, Jesus suffered and gained sympathy for us. He knows what it is to be tempted by anger. He knows what it is to be tempted to entertain wrong thoughts and wrong motives. He has sympathy for us—a *clear and complete* idea of what it's like to live in a human body. Jesus was the Son of Man as well as the Son of God.

The One sitting at the right hand of God is able to run to the aid of those who are tempted. What kind of aid? He prays for us. He who is highest in heaven, who died for us, now sits in heaven mentioning us *by name* to God!

Picture your Savior, best Friend, and Lord sitting at the right hand of God waiting to pray those requests. Becoming conscious of Jesus' office of intercession for you will increase your faith. It will also change how you word your prayers. It's not what you know, it is *Who* you know.

While praying for a lady after church one Sunday night, I took her hand and said, "Let's pray in tongues a second." As I stood there praying in tongues, I thought, Jesus wants this prayer answered more than I do, and He is holier than I am. He is perfect and ever lives to make intercession for us. I knew that the Holy Spirit had been born in me as an intercessor.

If the Intercessor inside of me is praying what the Intercessor is praying at the right hand of God, then I will get an answer to prayer.

I took hold of that lady's hand and began to pray. The first three or four sentences Ernie prayed. Then, suddenly, I realized that I had reached a different level and was praying in agreement with Jesus. Tears began to flow as I realized a miracle would occur because the High Priest and I were praying the same thing.

The Power Of Confession

Up to this point, I have laid a foundation for considering the following verse:

> Therefore, holy brethren, partakers of the heavenly calling, consider the Apostle and High Priest of our confession, Christ Jesus—Hebrews 3:1.

Jesus is the High Priest of *our* confession, not *His* confession! Whatever we speak, He turns to the Father and prays. We affect what Jesus prays for us by what comes out of our mouth!

Perhaps you get up each morning and say, "I don't have any joy. I'm tired of it all. Life's a merry-go-round; which horse am I going to ride today?" Jesus, who spilled His own blood for you, will turn to His Father and say, "I can't pray that."

Why not get out of bed and say, "The Bible says that the Lord is my strength, my shield, my fortress, and my high tower. I'm complete in Him, and I don't care what I feel like! All that Christ Jesus is lives in me." That will make the High Priest sitting at the right hand of God get excited and say, "Did you hear what he said? Father, be his strength. Be his shield. Be his fortress and his joy." When Jesus turns to the Father and prays that prayer, the Father releases it, and the Holy Spirit pours it out on you.

Jesus is the High Priest of what you speak. You determine what He prays for you by your own confession, as long as the confession is clearly scriptural.

This concept is also outlined in Proverbs 18:20-21:

> A man's belly shall be satisfied with the fruit of his mouth; and with the increase of his lips shall he be filled. Death and life are in the power of the tongue: and they that love it shall eat the fruit thereof—*KJV*.

If you speak it, you have to eat it. You spread the table of your life with your own mouth. If you begin to increase what you speak, you will increase what you receive. If you begin to speak faith and joy, Jesus will become the High Priest of what you have spoken. He will pray what you confess.

6

PETITIONING THE KING THROUGH OBEDIENCE

Now that we have discussed transferal, let's consider another problem associated with prayer—that of finding God's will. 1 John 5:14-15 says,

> Now this is the confidence that we have in Him, that if we ask anything according to His will, He hears us. And if we know that He hears us, whatever we ask, we know that we have the petitions that we have asked of Him.

These verses tell us that if our requests are according to the Lord's will, then He hears us. And if He hears us, He will grant the petition. It is a three-fold process: 1) we ask according to His will; 2) He hears us; and 3) He answers our prayers.

An old saying states that there are three answers to every prayer: "yes," "no," and "wait." That is a nice little ditty, but I do not think it is true.

This particular scripture says that if God hears us, we have the petition. The implication is that if our prayers are not answered, God never heard them.

Nothing is wrong with God, and nothing is wrong with God's desire to hear and answer prayer. He is not an unwilling God who has to have His arm twisted. God *wants* to answer our prayers. Our problem, then, is that we present all kinds of petitions that have nothing to do with the will or the purposes of God.

The Seer Principle

Notice that all prayer has to start with God's will. According to 1 John, our confidence is in the fact that we ask *according to His will.* Therefore, the first order of business in praying is not talking but listening. After reading the scriptures, the first step is getting a word of wisdom or a word of knowledge concerning our prayers rather than bombarding heaven to coerce, twist, and force our human wisdom—or more accurately, our *lack* of wisdom—on God. We need to pray until we know God's will. Then, if we pray according to God's will, He will hear us; because He hears us, we will have the petition.

To illustrate this concept, let's turn to the Gospel of John. Chapter five records the story of Jesus' encounter with a man who had lain sick at the pool of Bethesda for thirty-eight years. After healing the man, Jesus was questioned by the religious leaders concerning His healing a man on the Sabbath. Jesus' explanation is found in verse nineteen:

> "Truly, truly, I say to you, the Son can do nothing of Himself, unless it is something He sees the Father doing; for whatever the Father does, these things the Son also does in like manner"—*NASB*.

I call this the "Seer Principle." A *seer* is one who sees.

Jesus was a seer and a prophet. We are to be seers, too, for we need to "see" what the Father is doing. Jesus Himself said He could do nothing of Himself. If the Lord Jesus could not heal this person unless the Father was healing him, then how much more must we say, "We can do nothing apart from the Father"?

A multitude of sick people lay at the pool, yet Jesus healed only one. Why did He do that? His explanation is, "I only saw the Father healing one person, and I moved with My Father."

He reiterates this idea in verse thirty of the same chapter:

> "I can do nothing on My own initiative. As I hear, I judge; and My judgment is just, because I do not seek My own will, but the will of Him who sent Me"—*NASB*.

If that condition is true for the Son of God, it certainly must be true for you and me. The key to prayer is to find out how heaven is moving and to line up with heaven. We must discover the direction of God.

Consider this concept in view of the literal translation of Matthew 16:19. The *New American Standard Bible* reads,

> "I will give you the keys of the kingdom of heaven; and whatever you shall bind on earth shall be bound in heaven, and whatever you shall loose on earth shall be loosed in heaven"—*NASB*.

The verbs *loosed* and *bound* in this verse are actually *perfect passive participles* in the Greek and are translated more accurately in the *Amplified Version*: "must be *already bound* in heaven" and "must be what is *already loosed* in heaven."

Whatever we bind must be bound in heaven. When heaven decides to release the antichrist, we can bind him until the cows come home. But because heaven is not binding him, he will not be bound. We do not control God through prayer— we move with Him in what He is already doing. The Lord once told me, "I will answer any prayer that Jesus is praying through you." Any prayer that comes out of our soulish realm is not going to be answered because it is not according to God's will;

He will not hear it. But if, on the other hand, I listen and receive a word of wisdom or a word of knowledge, I will pray His prayers and see them answered.

During the Iranian hostage crisis, I said, "Lord, I do not believe they will get out. I do not have any faith that they will get out. Please show me how to pray." (Honesty is another important ingredient in prayer.)

After about ten days of prayer, the Lord reminded me of Daniel chapter ten and said, "They will never get out until you do what Daniel did. You must proclaim a fast like Daniel's fast, committing yourself to twenty-one days of prayer and fasting in order to bind the Prince of Persia."

A few days later, the Lord told me that He would give me three hundred people to fast with me. And a few days after that, He told me He would give me nine hundred people if I would wax bold in faith. Nine hundred and fifty-two people from *Full Faith Church of Love* pledged to join me in a twenty-one day fast to bind the Prince of Persia. At that point, I knew the hostages would come home.

The point is that merely praying for God to force the release of the hostages would be fruitless. I first had to discern heaven's plan for that situation. True prayer is listening instead of simply shooting our guns off in the air. When we aim at nothing, we hit nothing.

On the other hand, the Bible says that if God listens to us, we will have our petition. That concept may grate us because it implies that He does not hear much of what you and I pray. But let's face it: many of our prayers simply do not get answered, which suggests that God never heard them in the first place.

Standing On The Word

If we can become attuned to God's will in our prayers, we can proceed with confidence. Let's turn to Isaiah 62:6-7 for guidance in how to proceed.

> On your walls, O Jerusalem, I have appointed watchmen; all day and night they will never keep silent. You who remind the Lord, take no rest for yourselves; and give Him no rest until He establishes and makes Jerusalem a praise in the earth—*NASB.*

Although the specific context of this scripture is a prayer for Jerusalem, the principle is true across the board that we are to "remind the Lord" and "give Him no rest" until His promise is realized. Once we have a word from God concerning a promise, we can approach Him saying, "Lord, You said. . . . Lord, you wrote. . . ."

For example, in the hostage situation, we took hold of Daniel 10 and reminded the Lord; and we stayed with that scripture.

Once we have a scripture that applies to our situation—once God gives us a word, particularly a word in *the* Word—then we can take hold of it, stand on it, and pray it. We can say, "Lord, You said that if I ask anything according to Your will, You will grant it. Here it is, and I am reminding You."

This theme of reminding God is also evident in Isaiah 43:26, where the Lord exhorts us to put Him "in remembrance; let us argue our case together, state your cause, that you may be proved right" (*NASB*).

Too often we have no case. The Lord then responds with, "What scripture are you basing your prayer on?"; or, "Are you willing to get out of the sin that has created your problem?"; or, "You are under the chastisement of God, and it will not be lifted."

We need to understand our case. We need to know what we are doing before we come before God. Remember, Jesus said not to use "vain repetitions as the heathen do" (Matthew 6:7). It is not how *much* we pray—it is how *accurately* we pray. In the Sermon on the Mount, He tells us to avoid using many words when we pray. The key to prayer is listening to find whether we have a case.

What would be your argument to God that Nicaragua could be spared from Castro's domination? Do you have a case? Do you have any scriptural basis to snatch Nicaragua away from communism?

Do you think America should be spared? If you go before God and say, "I am claiming that America will escape World War III," you may not have a case. You cannot simply show up in heaven and command God, as if you were God and He were your servant. It is impossible to be strong in prayer if we are not strong in the Scripture. (See Isaiah 41:26.)

Four Levels Of Rebellion

This concern for the Scripture implies an obedient reverence for its authority. Most Christians are not serious about obedience. They believe in obedience in theory, but when it comes down to verses that disagree with their lives, they say, "That does not apply to me."

Consider the divorce rate among believers. A Christian husband or wife should not even mention divorce. If they are serious about God, how could they even consider divorce as an option or alternative? A believer cannot help it if his or her spouse leaves. But that circumstance aside, thousands of Christians are getting divorces today. Apparently, the Bible has no effect or influence in their lives; all their obedience is in theory.

Also, if one takes obedience seriously, he could not marry an unbeliever. If he took obedience seriously, he would have to tithe. Many people do not even pray about tithing—the Bible says to *do* it. If a woman takes obedience seriously, she could not have an abortion; it would not be an option, for she could not even consider it.

It distresses me how few Christians actually accept the Bible as authoritative. Most Christians think it is authoritative until it crosses them—at that point they throw away the Bible. Their obedience is not practical or actual but theoretical.

The Lord gave me a vision concerning disobedience as I was praying for the Church. In this vision, I saw a basement strewn with crumbs, trash, and garbage. I knew I could not clean it because it was too dirty and filthy. Then I saw that the next level down was a pit. The third level down contained a false light, and the fourth level down was a lake of fire.

Then the word of the Lord came to me, and I began to understand the vision: Some people are disobedient and have stepped down, spiritually, into a filthy basement. It is full of garbage, roaches, rats, tin cans, banana peels, and all kinds of partially decayed food. That basement is where these disobedient persons are "at" today. It is a perfect description of their spiritual condition.

The only way to treat such a basement is to move out of it. It cannot be "cleaned." Anyone in it will simply have to get out. If you are in that basement, you have got to *get out*. If you are having an affair, get out of it. If you are an alcoholic, throw away the booze.

If you don't get out of that filthy basement, you go down into level two: a pit of sorrow, shame, anguish, depression, and mental problems. You can call it schizophrenia, or you can call it by Freudian terms—your problem will still be sin.

The third level contained a false light, which represents deception. This is the devil saying, "Sin is fun. It's all right to commit adultery, shoot up dope, and get drunk. Everybody else does."

Believers must be different—we must be a "peculiar people." We are different because we believe in Jesus' teachings and have absolutes. We have standards, and we will not compromise.

When I saw the fourth level down, I saw the light that was lighting the third level. It was emanating from the fire that burned in hell. Those living in perpetual, willful sin manifest that they are not really saved because they refuse to repent.

To escape those four levels—the ghetto basement, the pit of sorrow, the area of false light, and the lake of fire—flee from sin. Pray *until* you are free.

Abiding In Jesus

Let us examine this concept of obedience in John chapter fifteen, beginning in verse four: "Abide in Me, and I in you." The word *abide* is derived from a Greek word meaning "to live," "to dwell," or "to remain." For purposes of this discussion, I am going to use the word *remain* in our translation of this Greek word.

> "*Remain* in Me, and I in you. As the branch cannot bear fruit of itself, unless it *remains* in the vine, so neither can you, unless you *remain* in Me. I am the vine, you are the branches; he who *remains* in Me, and I in him, he bears much fruit; for apart from Me you can do nothing. If anyone does not *remain* in Me, he is thrown away as a branch, and dries up; and they gather them, and cast them into the fire, and they are burned. If you *remain* in Me, and My words *remain* in you, ask whatever you wish, and it shall be done for you"— John 15:4-7 *NASB, Italics added*.

Our first prayer request should be to abide in Christ. What does it mean to abide in Christ? It means that you have no willful sin, no bitterness toward any person, no one left unforgiven, no wrong relationship, no lust, no pornography, etc. To abide in Christ—to *remain* in Christ—is to remain in the Spirit. That means, as far as you know, there is nothing in your life that displeases Jesus. If you do not start praying about obedience, you are just *playing games about prayer!*

71

One real reason we do not have our prayers answered is found in John 15:7: "If you remain in Me, and My words [the Scripture] remain in you, ask whatever you wish, and it shall be done for you." We must go back to basics. We must start all over again: "Lord, my prayer is that I might be serious about obedience."

The opposite of abiding is living in an uncleanable basement: "I'll allow just a little sin here, a little anger there, a little beer in the refrigerator here, a few cuss words there, a dirty story here, some cheating on my income tax there. *I wonder where God is? How come He never hears me?*"

I did not get this out of a sermon illustration book. I got this praying for my church in the middle of the night. I realized that our first prayer request must be, "Jesus, I want to abide in you. I want to be filled with love, joy, peace, patience, gentleness, goodness, faith, meekness, and self-control. I want the glory of God on my face again. I want Your presence."

The Lord our God is one Lord. If you have two lords, He is not Lord. You need to pray earnestly, "I shall love the Lord my God with *all my heart* (plans, motives—no plans except God's plans). I shall love the Lord my God with *all my soul* (my emotions directed completely to Jesus). I shall love the Lord my God with *all my mind* (wholesome, pure thoughts). I shall love the Lord my God with *all my strength.*"

If you want to pray an excellent prayer, pray John 15:4. "I want to abide in You, Lord, because apart from You I can do nothing, *including* getting an answer to prayer."

I said earlier that we should remind the Lord by praying the Scripture. Begin to pray, "Lord, I choose to pay attention to Your commandments. I want well-being, peace like a river, and righteousness like the waves of the sea." (See Isaiah 48:17-18.) If we want peace, we must be obedient.

In Isaiah 59:5, the Lord tells us of those who "hatch adders' eggs and weave the spider's web; he who eats of their eggs dies, and from that which is crushed a snake breaks forth" (*NASB*). How can anyone pray who has adder's eggs or spider's webs in his heart? Do you have any living spiders? You must crush them. Do you have any little snakes? You had better kill them and start walking down the road of holiness.

Isaiah 63:10 is one of the most frightening verses in the Old Testament:

> But they rebelled and grieved His Holy Spirit; therefore, He turned Himself to become their enemy, He fought against them—*NASB*.

I would sure hate to rebel against and grieve the Holy Spirit until He turned, became my enemy, and fought against me.

I know people who have grieved the Holy Spirit through bitterness, hatred, and rebellion. Now the Holy Spirit is opposing them because they are walking in paths of sin. Instead of living under the blessing of God, they are under the woe of God. The Holy Spirit has become their enemy, and they have real problems. For that reason, Christians had better decide to be rebellious—against the devil!

Isaiah 65:2 also talks about disobedience, but it contains some good news:

> "I have spread out My hands all day
> long to a rebellious people, who walk
> in the way which is not good, follow-
> ing their own thoughts"—*NASB*.

God spreads out His hands even to those who are rebellious! And why does He want you to be obedient? He wants you to walk in a way that is good instead of a way that will hurt you.

Living Sacrifices

Finally, let's turn to a New Testament verse that I read in my own quiet time:

> And He went a little beyond them,
> and fell to the ground, and began to pray
> that if it were possible, the hour might
> pass Him by. And He was saying, "Abba!

> Father! All things are possible for Thee;
> remove this cup from Me; yet not what
> I will, but what Thou wilt''—Mark
> 14:35-36 *NASB*.

Jesus said these words in the Garden of Gethsemane. He could not escape Calvary and be obedient. His flesh (His emotions, His mind, and His will) did not want to go to Calvary. But He obeyed the Holy Spirit instead of His soulish realm. There was never a time when He allowed His flesh to be in rebellion against the Holy Spirit.

But it is important to realize that Jesus could have been disobedient had He not spent time in prayer. You and I will always be disobedient if we do not pray. In verses 37-38, He found His disciples sleeping and exhorted them to ''keep watching and praying, that you may not come into temptation; the spirit is willing, but the flesh is weak''—*NASB*.

Jesus learned this truth Himself as He was facing Calvary. He had just learned that the spirit was willing, but the flesh was weak. Nevertheless, He went to the cross the next day because He had won the victory the night before on His knees and His face. Therefore, He had victory the next day.

Would you like to have your flesh crucified every day? The spirit is willing, but the flesh is weak. To crucify your flesh, keep watch with Him one hour each morning. If you will spend an hour with God, you will have the Spirit in control instead of the flesh. Have an appointment with God!

We need to be one of those people who obey the Scripture, not theoretically but actually. Our number one priority in prayer should be, "Oh, God, I want to abide! I don't want to live in a ghetto basement. I want to live in the Spirit."

It is God's will that you abide; therefore, if you pray to abide, He will hear you, and you will have the petition. Get serious about obedience, and when the chips are down, you will crucify your flesh just as the Savior did.

7

HOW TO RELEASE THE POWER OF THE SPIRIT

Our number one weakness is not sin but prayerlessness. We do not pray enough for our families or our loved ones. The devil works overtime to keep us griping and complaining, but God does not have any crying towels. We need to pray.

> The Spirit also helps in our weaknesses. For we do not know what we should pray for as we ought, but the Spirit Himself makes intercession for us with groanings which cannot be uttered. Now He who searches the hearts knows what the mind of the Spirit is, because He makes intercession for the saints according to the will of God—Romans 8:26-27.

The apostle Paul includes himself when he says *we* do not know how to pray as we ought. If you say to yourself, "I don't know how to pray," I have good news for you: Neither did Paul! And neither do I.

Scripture says that the Holy Spirit makes intercession with groanings that cannot be uttered. In other words, the solution is not learning *how to pray* but *beginning* to pray. If you will begin to pray, the Lord will teach you how.

The Holy Spirit intercedes for us according to the will of God. He was born in you for that purpose. He is a prayer warrior, and He lives in you—a holy intercessor. That's good news.

Keys To Intercession

The Holy Spirit prays perfect prayers. Can you see, then, that the gift of tongues is a key to prayer? Tongues is especially important when followed by the gift of interpretation because the Holy Spirit inside of you, praying in words that you cannot understand, will then drop the meaning into your mind. What helps me more than anything else after a time of praying in tongues is sitting silently before the Lord. Then I can hear the voice of God giving me the right prayer to pray.

Hebrews 7:25 tells us that Jesus also lives to make intercession for us. We have, therefore, an intercessor inside (the Holy Spirit) and an intercessor at the right hand of God (the Lord Jesus). The key to prayer is the Holy Spirit praying in agreement with what Jesus is praying in heaven.

The implication of all that I have said is that *we were born again to pray*. The Holy Spirit has been born inside of us to pray perfect prayers. When we begin to pray in the Spirit, we will begin to realize answers to our prayers.

In a previous chapter, I discussed the concept of presenting our case before God and reminding Him of His promises. Isaiah 43:26 says, "Put Me in remembrance; let us argue our case together, state your cause, that you may be proved right" (*NASB*).

Notice that this verse mentions the word *argue*. It may be hard to identify prayer with arguing with God. Nevertheless, He encourages us to argue: " 'Present your case,' the Lord says. 'Bring forward your strong arguments,' the King of Jacob says" (Isaiah 41:21 *NASB*).

To illustrate, let's consider Exodus 33. Chapter thirty-two describes the children of Israel making the golden calf and God's subsequent anger. Upon his arrival with the Ten Commandments, Moses also became angry, destroyed the tablets, ground the golden idol into powder, and mixed the powder into a stream from which he made the people drink. He was as angry as God was.

God said,

> "I will send My Angel before you, and I will drive out the Canaanite and the Amorite and the Hittite and the Perizzite and the Hivite and the Jebusite.

Go up to a land flowing with milk and honey; for I will not go up in your midst, lest I consume you on the way, for you are a stiff-necked people'—Exodus 33:2-3.

In effect, God was saying, "I'm going to send an angel, but I am upset with you because you are stiff-necked, stubborn, and rebellious. If I went along with you, I might get so mad that I wipe all you turkeys out."

Then Moses began to pray,

"See, You say to me, 'Bring up this people.' But You have not let me know whom You will send with me. Yet You have said, 'I know you by name, and you have also found grace in My sight.'

"Now therefore, I pray, if I have found grace in Your sight, show me now Your way, that I may know You and that I may find grace in Your sight. And consider that this nation is Your people."

And He said, "My Presence will go with you, and I will give you rest."

Then he [Moses] said to Him, "If Your Presence does not go with us, do not bring us up from here"—Exodus 33:12-15.

Moses stated his case and presented his arguments. I don't know if this passage strikes you as funny, but it actually makes me laugh. In substance, Moses said, "Hey, God, I'm supposed to be Your favorite; You know me by name. Well, I want to tell You something: these are Your people, and You're copping out! And don't push off some angel on me. If You're not going, I'm not going." And he persuaded God to change His mind.

The Power Of God's Presence

Moses did exactly what Isaiah commanded: "Present your case; present your strong arguments." How would you like to lead the children of Israel without the presence of God? The presence of God is everything. What is a worship service without the presence of God? Nothing but religion! What is a marriage without the presence of God? It could be hell on earth.

I once performed a wedding in our church for a poor family that wasn't able to spend a great deal on a fancy ceremony. Only about twenty people attended. There was no wedding dress or tuxedo. I think the bride may have had one flower. During the ceremony, we had communion, and the Spirit of God came down.

Our janitor came in and sat in the back row. After the wedding, he said, "I've been to the biggest weddings in the church, but the presence of God was powerful at this one!"

God can show up at a nice, fancy wedding, too—my daughters have had nice weddings—but if God is not there, you do not have anything. That's the point: *His presence makes all the difference!*

Consider God's presence in the context of Jesus' statements about the Kingdom of God. He said that of those born of women, there had been none greater than John the Baptist; yet the least in the Kingdom is greater than John. (See Matthew 11:11.)

Every believer is greater than Moses, Abraham, David, the prophets, and the kings of Israel. Why? Because every believer, including you, has been born of God and has the Intercessor living inside—the Holy Spirit Himself. Neither Moses nor Abraham had Him. And God invites us to come, state our case, and present our strong arguments. Call on the Lord. Tell God if you think something's unfair. Get the Bible out and pray through the scriptures.

Notice how boldly Moses prayed. Maybe you have a wayward son, daughter, mother, or father. Why don't you take hold of the story of the Prodigal Son and say, "God, this is what Your Word says, and I'm going to pray that my loved one will come to the end of himself, tire of the pigpen he's in, and return home. I want this to happen for my boy." Present your case.

Another illustration, found in Genesis, concerns an uncle and a nephew. The uncle knew how to pray:

The Lord said, "Because the outcry against Sodom and Gomorrah is great, and because their sin is very grievous, I will go down now and see whether they have done altogether according to the outcry against it that has come to Me; and if not, I will know." Then the men [angels] turned away from there and went toward Sodom, but Abraham still stood before the Lord—Genesis 18:20-22.

In effect, Abraham said, "God, I know those are angels, but I'm not through yet. You and I must talk about this situation. I've got a nephew named Lot living in Sodom." So he remained standing and argued his case before the Lord while the angels went to Sodom.

Will you and I remain standing before the Lord when everybody else says there is no hope? When we engage God in conversation, things change.

Abraham asked the Lord, "Would You also destroy the righteous with the wicked? Suppose there were fifty righteous within the city" (Genesis 19:23-24). God's response was that He would spare the city for fifty righteous people. Abraham asked again about forty-five, then forty, thirty, twenty, and finally ten. God's response was that He would spare the city for the sake of ten righteous people.

Ten could not be found, so God destroyed Sodom and Gomorrah; but first He sent angels to allow Lot and his family to escape the judgment. Why? Because Abraham interceded for them. The angel was forced to say, "Hurry, escape . . . for I cannot do anything until you arrive there" (Genesis 19:22).

Do you realize the significance of that sentence? An angel of God, a supernatural being, said, "Because Abraham has prayed and touched God, my hand is held." Wouldn't you love to have an Uncle Abraham? Actually, most of us have had an uncle, a mother, a father, or an aunt who interceded for our salvation. We are not saved because we are more special than anyone else. We are saved because someone interceded and touched God for us.

Practical Intercession

I remember going to a small town to preach. The Spirit fell, and many wonderful things happened. Several people were filled with the Spirit and healed. Just when I thought I was something special, three ladies came up to me and said, "We have been praying every day for three years for an outpouring of the Holy Spirit in this church." It was not the preacher who caused that revival but the intercessors. *Prayer* moves the hand of God.

Some time ago, I was praying about the Supreme Court's support of abortion. I had been praying

Psalm 119:126 for two years: "It is time for You to act, for they have regarded Your law as void."

Almost daily I would say, "God, You said that it's time for You to move. I agree; it *is* time for You to move. They say it's okay to kill babies, so it's time for You to remove some justices."

Finally, at a prayer meeting, I said, "Lord, it's obvious that You're not hearing me."

The Lord answered, "You are praying about people; the problem is a demonic principality. The forces of hell are controlling the U.S. Supreme Court, and they will not move without fasting and prayer. I am not going to answer your prayer, the Supreme Court will not change, and America will not change unless somebody fasts and prays."

The problem with abortion is not people but a demonic principality: "We wrestle not against flesh and blood, but against principalities, against powers, against the rulers of the darkness of this world" (Ephesians 6:12 *KJV*).

Later, while I was praying, the Lord told me that the satanic claw over the Supreme Court would be moved when we moved the thumb. At a city-wide pastor's meeting, the Lord told another pastor that the thumb of that claw is the spirit of lawlessness.

This entire country has been built on lawlessness and rebellion. I am not condemning the Revolutionary War, but we must admit that the United States was founded through revolution. The spirit of America cries out, "I don't have to obey anybody! I don't have to be under authority; I'll do *what* I want to do, *when* I want to do it, and the *way* I want to do it!"

The word "antichrist" in the Bible is the Greek word "lawlessness." When the Bible says that the Antichrist is the son of iniquity, the Greek literally means that he is the *"son of lawlessness."*

Can you see how lawlessness is connected with humanism? If man is the center of all things—if man is the measure of all things—we do not need God. But those assumptions are steeped in rebellion. Humanism is only a symptom of a spirit of lawlessness, and that spirit is in the church, too. It hovers over all of us. We must hate rebellion in ourselves and love obedience to the Word of God.

God will speak to us if we will go to Him for direction. If we state our case and listen for His answer, He will show us how to pray according to His knowledge and will. We can fast against the principality of lawlessness because God has revealed that it is at the root of the abortion issue. Had He not revealed it, we would still be praying against people.

If Moses and Abraham could get God talking— and if we are under a better covenant than they, with better promises and the indwelling Holy Spirit—how much more can we do the same thing?

Can you see from these illustrations what it means to state your case before God? Can you see the importance of getting a Word from God's

Scripture and presenting it to Him? You must get Him to talk, and you must listen. Then you will be able to take hold of a verse and pray effectively.

Effects Of Criticism

Let's consider one final point about intercession with a story from the twelfth chapter of Numbers. Miriam and Aaron criticized Moses because of a woman he married. They said, in effect, "You think you are the only spiritual one. God speaks to us just as much as He speaks to you." God said in return, "Come down to the tent of meeting." When they arrived, He said, "I speak to Moses face to face." Then He struck Miriam with leprosy.

Leprosy is symbolic of gossip. In the first place, leprosy is terminal, and anyone who gossips has a terminal disease. Leprosy is also contagious, and gossips are dangerous. Finally, leprosy isolates its victims. Lepers were forced to live apart from the rest of the community and wear a lip covering. Everywhere lepers went, they were instructed by God to cry, "Unclean! Unclean! I am unclean!"

Similarly, every negative, critical, slandering person should have a cloth over his lip. Everywhere he goes he should say, "I am unclean. Watch out for me or you will contract a terminal disease!"

Gossips are always on the way out of a church. When someone begins to be a slanderer, he may not have *decided* to leave, but he is on his way to cutting himself off from the the assembly.

In Miriam's case, however, Moses cried out to God for his sister. He prayed. He stated his case and tried to temper God's judgment. Isn't it beautiful for a leader like Moses to love his sister so much? Although God forced her to remain outside the camp for seven days, He then healed her. Miriam was spared, but the nation of Israel had to wait an entire week for her to be healed.

That story is a picture of righteous leadership. One of the hardest people to pray for is that person who criticizes. Every person alive has been criticized by his family, a friend, or someone else. That statement is particularly true for leaders. We are all bound to receive criticism, but the righteous response is to pray for the leper.

God's Word says, "Bless those who curse you, and pray for those who spitefully use you" (Luke 6:28). If you are wondering what has hindered your prayers, the Lord may remind you that you have some enemies that you must love with the love of God. Their criticism may be unjust, and they may say all kinds of evil things about you. Nevertheless, one of the most important keys to prayer is the love of God.

If you want to do business with God, then you must love your enemies. You must love the Miriams. This story is not based on a theoretical situation—it is about two brothers and a sister who were not getting along. One of them found herself under judgment, and the righteous one in the bunch released her from that judgment.

If a family squabble occurs and you are in the right, it is still *your* job to intercede. You must let the Holy Spirit inside you pray, and you must place yourself back in the love of God. Then you can free your family from leprosy.

A funeral director once told me that major conflicts surface among family members in 80 percent of the funerals he conducts. I said, "It couldn't be that high!"

He said, "You ought to hear them come in and argue; they are already fighting over the goodies before they get the corpse in the grave." His statement tells me that this message is important: We must pray for the Miriams.

Are you willing to pray for the Miriam in your house this week, whoever she (or he) may be? Are you willing to pray for the Supreme Court? Are you willing to put this principle into practice when you present your case to the Lord?

You will often find that God does not answer your prayer because He wants to talk to you first. Once you let Him tell you where you are praying and looking at things incorrectly—and where you need to begin to pray—you will see your prayers answered.

In all of our binding and loosing, the first thing we must concern ourselves with is what needs to be bound and loosed in *our own lives*. If we can remove the evil spirits from ourselves and loose the right attitudes into ourselves, then we will be able to effect changes in other people's lives.

8

AVOIDING PRESUMP-
TION IN PRAYER

God has created two realms of authority—the heavenly realm and the earthly realm. The heavenly realm may also be termed God's realm, the spiritual realm, or the eternal realm. The earthly realm may in turn be called the human realm, the natural realm, or the temporal realm.

The heavenly realm contains what we have potentially, and the earthly realm contains what we have actually received. These distinctions demonstrate a basic problem in the Christian life: *that which is spiritually, eternally given in is not necessarily received or manifested in our lives.*

Psalm 115:16 tells us that "the heavens are the Lord's, but the earth He has given to the children of men." According to this verse, God rules in heaven. But who actually rules over this earth? Satan is the prince of the power of this world. When man sinned in the garden, he rebelled against God Almighty and gave Satan authority over the earthly realm. Mankind traded gods.

Through prayer, however, we Christians can rule in this realm: "the earth he has given to the children of men." It is the Church's responsibility to rule! God has given the earth to us, and we have to move the Kingdom of God from heaven to earth. This is why Jesus prayed, "Thy kingdom come. Thy will be done, on earth as it is in heaven" (Matthew 6:10 *KJV*).

God has control of the heavens, but man has control of the earth. War, suffering, and sin exist because we have not released the Kingdom, authority, and power of God in this lower realm.

This principle is in operation even in our praises. Psalm 149:6 instructs us to "let the high praises of God be in [our] mouth, and a two-edged sword in [our] hand." High praise is when praise on the earthly realm is in harmony with praise in the heavenly realm. When we begin to worship in the same way and in the same spirit as the angels, then our praise is no longer earthly praise and worship. Our praises have become high praises because they match the praise in heaven. Praise becomes a two-edged sword that pulls down demonic influences in the heavenlies.

Every request has to be *received before it is prayed*. Prayer involves letting God talk. Therefore, we must be listening all the time. It is impossible to talk without ceasing, but we can listen without ceasing. Listening to what is coming down from the heavenly realm is the key to praying without ceasing.

Praying in tongues is a wonderful way to find out what is on God's heart, if we pray for an interpretation. God's will may come by an impression, a vision, a dream, a word of knowledge, or a scripture. However it comes, we have received God's request from the spiritual realm.

Praise and worship are beautiful avenues for discovering what is on God's heart. Worship and praise can tune us in to what is important to Him. As the believer tunes in to God through worship, he will often find that what he should do about his job, his marriage, his son, his daughter, etc. has dropped into his mind.

Having received the request, we have solved two problems: knowing what God's will is and the problem of praying in faith. When we hear a word, we know God's will. And having heard God's voice, we have faith given to us. When God speaks to us, we do not have any difficulty believing. We then cooperate with heaven by returning the request. Intervention in the earthly, temporal realm can only come as the result of some form of prayer. Prayer in some form—tongues, listening, worship, thanksgiving, adoration, petition—is the *only means of releasing God's intervention on earth.*

I cannot overemphasize the importance of prayer or the importance of knowing God's heart when we pray. "Who is he who speaks and it comes to pass, when the Lord has not commanded it?" (Lamentations 3:37). It is vain to confess in the earthly realm what God has not commanded in the heavenly realm. We can say it a thousand times, but if God has not commanded it, it is vain.

Before we confess, we need to find out what God's heart is. If you read the Bible constantly, you have a pretty good shot at knowing what God's heart is.

One thing the Lord does not need is an abundance of words when we pray. Instead of praying six hours, we might be better off listening for five minutes. We must understand the prayer request that is on God's heart.

Cooperation And Presumption

Prayer always requires cooperation between God and man. We cannot do God's part, and He will not do our part. God's role is to initiate His purpose and plan. We cannot initiate God's will. Our part is to discover what God's will is and to ask according to His will.

Every miracle, salvation, and baptism in the Holy Spirit is the result of cooperation between God and man. *Prayer is our harmonizing with heaven*.

Presumption is demanding God to act according to *our* will before we receive a request from Him. Presumption produces unbelief because such prayers are not answered. Most prayer requests come out of the soulish, human realm and thus remain unanswered. People who presume ignore what conditions have to be met and what scriptural principles are operating. What is on God's heart may be completely different from what is on our heart.

If a person has migraine headaches, he may say, "I know God's will is for me to be healed. I confess that I am healed!" Nothing happens. The prayer is not answered. What's wrong? Presumption never considers conditions or spiritual principles.

If that person were to get down on his face before God, the Lord might say, "Hey, you need to forgive forty people. Don't ask Me to take away your migraine headaches; ask Me to take away your bitterness and resentment." The person is praying about the headache, but heaven will not hear him because the headache is not the issue. He has an unanswered prayer because he is demanding God to do something without first hearing what God wants. That is presumption!

Presumption never considers conditions. We show up and start ordering God. If we would dare ask God what is wrong with our prayer life and wait for the answer, He might say, "You are sinning against the wife of your youth" or "You have resentment toward that child."

Recently, an elderly lady showed me a picture of a little china doll. She said, "That is the only doll I owned, and I had to share it with my whining little sister. And she broke it."

"Have you ever forgiven her?" I asked.

"No, I really haven't," she said.

How many "No, I really haven'ts" are there in your life? It can block prayer.

Presumption ignores conditions and spiritual principles, ignores what is on God's heart, and ultimately causes unbelief. When we name and claim and do not receive what we have claimed, we believe something is wrong with God. "I followed the formulas. I did it three hundred days in a row, and nothing happened."

Many people feel that way. You may even be one of them. But nothing is wrong with the Bible, God, or His love for you. *The problem is that you are demanding God to do something different than what is on His heart.*

Tailor-Made Prayers

Sometimes we get an answer to prayer by accident. This is true because some things are clearly God's will. We pray without listening or waiting, yet we receive an answer because what we have prayed is clearly His will, at least in general terms. But why not make a *tailor-made* prayer in Jesus' name?

For example, if someone is praying for a lost person, he knows God's will is for everyone to be saved. Why would he need to listen to God? There's a world of difference between praying for: A) a woman who was abused during childhood and as a result of that abuse has had a list of sordid affairs; hates men; hates sex; and cannot relate to marriage; B) a teenager who was made to go to church, made to worship, and has parents who criticize him with, "You didn't have your hands up. You're missing out with God. You start worshipping God"; C) a man who never once in his life knew a Christian man that he respected. Those are three different creatures, and they demand three different prayer requests.

For the third person, God might say in a word of wisdom to pray for a man to come into his life who is full of Jesus—a man whom he can respect. As a result of that relationship, he will receive Jesus. If the believer received that as a word from the Lord, he would be praying specifically.

For the woman who has been abused, hurt, and wounded, the Lord might say, "Pray that she will find a Christian lady who will sit down with her, work through these things, and sort out her problems without condemnation or judgment."

For the teenager, the believer might find himself praying, "Cause that father to go to that son and apologize for cramming *churchianity* and religion at him until he rebelled against the Lord."

It is not enough to say, "I know it is God's will that this person or that person be saved. We must get to the heart of the situation and pray a tailor-made prayer. God is the tailor.

Do not be discouraged. God loves to answer prayer. But the prayer must always be received before it is prayed by us. We must receive the request from the spiritual realm, and then we must pray it back to God. When we receive a word from Him, we know our prayer will be answered, for it agrees with God.

9

TWELVE ARENAS OF CONFLICT

Christianity involves and demands conflict, and believers face obstacles in many different arenas throughout their lives. Jesus hasn't left us without the means to face these trials, however, as this passage from Matthew proves:

> When Jesus reached the district of Caesarea Philippi, He asked His Disciples, "Who do people say that the Son of Man is?" They answered, "Some say John the Baptist, some Elijah, others Jeremiah or one of the prophets."
> He said to them, "Who do you yourselves say that I am?"
> And Simon Peter answered, "You are the Christ, the Son of the living God."
> Then Jesus answered him, "Blessed are you, Simon, son of Jonah, for it is not man that made this known to you but my Father in Heaven. And I, yes I,

tell you, your name from now on is to be Peter, Rock, and on a massive rock like this I will build my church, and the powers of the underworld shall never overthrow it. I will give you the keys of the kingdom of heaven, and whatever you forbid on earth must be what is already forbidden in heaven, and whatever you permit on earth must be what is already permitted in heaven''— Matthew 16:13-19 *Williams*.

A popular song says, "Blow the trumpet in Zion" and "sound the alarm in the Holy mountain." Do you realize that the alarm *does* need to be sounded in the Church?

Unfortunately, many people have been overcome by the gates of hell and fallen flat on their faces. Marriages have collapsed, people have become alcoholics, and seemingly faithful spouses have entered into adultery. I know pastors who have ruined their ministries—men and women who once sought God wholeheartedly and were glorious testimonies. Somehow, they missed out with God because they did not watch and pray.

Binding And Loosing

If we are not careful, we begin to think God's blessings are automatic. But according to Matthew 16, a condition must be met to prevent the gates of hell from overpowering us. Two keys have been given to us by the Lord Jesus Christ, and if we don't use them, we're going to be in big trouble.

The two keys both concern prayer. One is *binding,* and the other is *loosing.* Having the keys in our pocket won't get the job done. We have to engage in some actual binding and loosing in every realm of life.

Notice that these particular verbs are *perfect passive participles.* The *Williams* translation says in a footnote that the verse refers to "things in a state of having been *already forbidden."* He goes on to say that "the Church in the New Order must act in accordance with the will of heaven." These two keys are not a blank check: we can only forbid what heaven is forbidding, and we can only loose what heaven is loosing.

As I read this passage, I saw various arenas of conflict: salvation, healing, obedience, Baptism in the Holy Spirit, finances, occupation, marriage, church, personal habits, parenting, our city, and our nation. Surrounding each one of these realms is a satanic force trying to keep us from receiving salvation, healing, etc. Demons work against our obedience, marriage, churches, and home groups. Satan attacks us in the area of habits, and he attacks our occupations. There is certainly satanic activity against the Baptism in the Holy Spirit.

When I talk about binding and loosing, I am not talking about some vague theory but practical Christianity. If you fail to bind and loose in your marriage, you can get into trouble very quickly. Perhaps your finances are under attack—maybe you are an impulse-buyer. Do you think impulsive buying is a natural thing? Could an evil spirit possibly influence you to spend money you don't have or charge items until something is your master besides *the* Master? Spiritual forces are at work!

Do you fail to pray for your children? Spiritual forces can keep you from crying out to God for your son or daughter. Do you fail to pray for your parents? Many parents are in serious trouble and in desperate need of prayer. You need to *use* the keys of binding and loosing. The devil is working against your obedience to pray.

Are you opposed to receiving the Baptism in the Holy Spirit? God wants you to have it! He does not want you to be half full. The Lord does not want you to go around saying, "Half and half."

When I was a denominational preacher, every Sunday I shook people's hands after the service, and they would say, "How are you today, Brother Ernie?" I always said, "Half and half." They would ask, "Half and half?" I would laugh and say, "Half milk, half cream—half sinner and half saint."

One Christmas night I got tired of having wrong thoughts, so I said, "I'm going to pray until I get hold of God's power." The Spirit of God came inside of me, and I gained victory for the first time in my life! Jesus said to me, "Now you do not have to say 'half and half' anymore. Out of the abundance of your heart your mouth was speaking."

If you are half and half, you need to get filled with the Holy Spirit. "If any man be in Christ he is a new creature! Old things have passed away (dirty movies, drinking, drugs); behold, all things have become new!" (See 2 Corinthians 5:17.)

If you have a problem in your finances—you are out of work, not getting paid enough money to keep up with your bills, or feel trapped in your vocation—you need to bind and loose. Once I had a vision of a demon holding the back pocket and billfold of a brother in my church. I bound that demon, and the brother got a promotion in two weeks.

If you have a financial need, bind every spirit of compulsive, foolish spending, greed, and lust for unnecessary things. Loose upon yourself a generous spirit, faith to tithe, and faith to give. Once you have faith to see those who have less than you, you can share. Loose the good hand of the Lord upon yourself for good in financial realms.

Start With Yourself

Years ago our church went through a time when every elders' meeting was a horror. We had only nitpicking and squabbling, and I could not understand the problem. We were used to unity, love, and joy. But now *everything* was going wrong, and everyone had a negative, critical attitude.

While out for a walk, I prayed in tongues. Suddenly I had a vision of a school playground. Little green imps with satanic grins were sliding down the slides, riding on the teeter-totters, and climbing on the monkey bars. I said, "Lord, what in the world does that mean?" He said, "You are the pastor, but you haven't been binding and loosing. Demons have made a playground out of your church."

Finally understanding the problem, I prayed, "You spirits of disunity, criticism, negativism, nit-picking, and backbiting, *I bind you in the name of Jesus!* You cannot work against or through me or any of our elders."

At the next elders' meeting, I found perfect peace, harmony, and love. Now I always bind and loose before each meeting. Once I even stopped the session and went for a walk because I forgot to bind and loose beforehand. After getting alone, I put the key of prayer into the door and did some powerful shouting in the devil's ear.

You might ask, "Who on the elder board gets under the control of an evil spirit?" Every man can get underneath a wrong spirit. I don't bind the demons from specific elders—I bind those demons from all of us.

We often make the mistake of binding and loosing for someone else instead of ourselves. What if I prayed, "I want to get my wife straightened out, and I am going to bind this or loose that." I would probably already be out of the Spirit.

If you want to do some binding and loosing, always start with yourself. Get the demons off your back, and get yourself straightened out. People who specialize in binding and loosing are often negative, looking at everybody else's problem: "How are we going to get all *their* demons bound up?"

Could it be that the devil has made a playground out of your marriage—your physical union or your communication? What's wrong with your marriage? Let me ask you a question: Have you bound or loosed anything in reference to your marriage in the last two months? Have you used these two keys? Jesus said that the gates of hell *will* prevail against you if you don't use the keys. If you haven't bound or loosed anything in two months, what can you expect?

You can have a whole cluster of demons operating around your family and your children. When the demons working on you get the other demons working on your kids, you can have a serious fight.

What I am talking about is real. There are demons, and they have to be bound, not just in one realm but in at least the twelve realms mentioned earlier. If you do not bind them, you are going to go broke or bankrupt. If you do not bind them, you might get a divorce or lose a child. Blessings are not automatic. Sound the trumpet in Zion! Blow the trumpet! "Bind and loose," the Lord says to you. In which realm have you failed to bind and loose?

The King's Standard

We need this message not because it is new intellectually but because we have to be reminded of who the enemy is. And we have to be reminded to act. God is not impressed that we know all about binding and loosing if we are not actually doing it.

Isaiah 54:17 encourages us:

> "No weapon formed against you shall prosper, and every tongue which rises against you in judgment you shall condemn. This is the heritage of the servants of the Lord, and their righteousness is from Me," says the Lord.

This verse is about warfare, and binding and loosing is warfare. Why don't you confess: "No weapon formed against me, my finances, my children, my pastor, my husband, or my wife shall prosper"?

Isaiah 59:19 says, "When the enemy comes in like a flood, the Spirit of the Lord will lift up a standard against him." Have you ever been in a flood of swirling waves, mud, and destruction? When the enemy comes, he comes like a flood. He attacks our children, our marriage, our finances, etc. But God says that "the Spirit of the Lord will lift up a standard against him."

We need to have a standard in the Church that says we will not speak badly of any other person. We need to determine that we will not go to divorce court. The Church needs a standard that says we do not need booze, beer, wine, pot, or cocaine. Then, when the enemy tries to come in like a flood, we can say, "Hey, we don't need that. We're happy without it." When someone slanders us, we can say, "Well, that's his problem. We only speak good of pastors, churches, national leaders, and one another because we have a standard."

The inference of this verse is that you have a standard—a great big ark of safety that you can climb into. You can say, "Let it rain; I'm in God's ark—the Lord Jesus Christ." If you are in the ark, you don't have to worry about the flood!

The Spirit of God is going to raise up holiness more and more—not a legalistic holiness but a practical holiness. He is going to establish things such as loving when everybody else is spiteful and mean.

Being part of the family of God is not the same as being in the army. We need warriors who will battle the enemy in the name of that standard.

A good friend of mine was an SAC pilot for years. Every time an alert came up on the screen, he took off and flew a B-52 halfway to Russia, assuming that "this was it." Outside the Russian radar was a certain line; and right before he crossed it, he would circle until the President of the United States said, "It is a false alert." He didn't wait until he found out before taking off. Time after time he flew toward Russia, not knowing whether this time he would go in and participate in a nuclear holocaust.

There is a big difference between being an American and being in the U.S. Army. The soldier's life is on the line. I had an uncle who served in Korea. During one fierce battle, the Chinese ran 100,000 soldiers at some rolls of barbed wire, even though their men were being killed almost immediately. Eventually, so many dead Chinese were caught in the wire that their fellow soldiers could climb over their bodies to the next roll. Firing continuously, my uncle watched his machine gun melt because it became so hot.

There is also a big difference between being in the family of God and being in the army of God. Those in the army fight to protect even those who are not fighting.

The army of God is made up of those who know how to bind and loose. They do the praying in the Church to keep everyone else safe; the rest of us loaf behind the lines.

Would you like to join the army of God? You will have to get out those two keys and start praying for your father, your mother, and your children. Pray for your church and its pastors. Bind and loose attitudes, influences, disunity, uncleanness, and worldliness. Loose hunger for prayer, intercession, fasting, and knowledge of the Word of God.

Binding The Strong Man

At a pastor's prayer meeting, the Lord showed us that the satanic principality over the United States Supreme Court is like a claw. The Lord said, "If you can get rid of the thumb, the devil will have to loosen his grip." The thumb of that hand is the *principality of lawlessness, rebellion, and independence*—the very same principality that is over America. Now we know what to pray for. We need to fast one day a week and pray against that principality of lawlessness, rebellion, and independence ("doing our own thing"). That spirit is a satanic principality over our nation. We will have to get that demon bound if we are going to save this country!

Mark 3:27 says, "No one can enter a strong man's house and plunder his goods, unless he first binds the strong man." We need to hear from heaven the strong man's name. We know the name of the strong man binding the United States of America and the Supreme Court, and now we can do business.

Do you know the strong man working in your office or against your finances? Do you know the strong man coming down your family tree? Do you know the name of the strong man behind your depression or your daughter's attitude? You need to pray in tongues until you receive a revelation and interpretation. You need to wait on the Lord.

You must bind whatever heaven is binding and loose whatever heaven is loosing. Keys are useless unless they are taken out and put in a door.

> Be strong in the Lord and in the power of His might. Put on the whole armor of God, that you may be able to stand against the wiles of the devil. For we do not wrestle against flesh and blood, but against principalities, against powers, against the rulers of the darkness of this age, against spiritual hosts of wickedness—Ephesians 6:10-12.

Pray and *wait* upon the Lord: "Lord Jesus, by the Holy Spirit, reveal to me what I need to bind and loose in each of arena of conflict:

1. Your own salvation
2. Healing—emotional/physical
3. Obedience and victory
4. Baptism in the Holy Spirit
5. Finances/spending
6. Your office/occupation
7. Your marriage (or others')
8. Your church—pastors/leaders
9. Parenting
10. Personal habits
11. Your city/local leaders
12. Your nation—Supreme Court/ President/Congress

Do not proceed to the next chapter until you are through binding and loosing, even if it takes several prayer sessions.

10

INTERNATIONAL INTERCESSION

Revelation 5:1-8 is a long, mysterious passage describing a heavenly book with seven seals. When these seals are opened, the imminent events associated with them are loosed to occur. And the only person worthy to open this scroll is the Lion of the tribe of Judah—Jesus Christ, the sovereign Lord of history.

How, then, is prayer important in the breaking of these seals? It is written that "the twenty-four elders fell down before the Lamb, each having a harp, and golden bowls full of incense, *which are the prayers of the saints*" (Revelation 5:8, *Italics added*). Prayer must be taken into account before the end-time events can occur.

If you think everything is predetermined, you are wrong. While the events of Revelation are predetermined, how they affect the people you pray for is not predetermined. Before any seal can be broken (and later on in the eighth chapter, before any trumpet can sound) heaven must first take into account all the prayers that have been prayed. The incense of prayer controls the destiny of individuals. While the events in history are predetermined, we can influence people's lives within those events and create "pockets of mercy" in their midst. Does that encourage you to pray for the United States and your loved ones? It should!

Now let's look at some scriptures that speak specifically about praying for our nation. 1 Timothy 2:1-6 says,

> Therefore I exhort first of all that supplications, prayers, intercessions, and giving of thanks be made for all men, for kings and all who are in authority, that we may lead a quiet and peaceable life in all godliness and reverence. For this is good and acceptable in the sight of God our Savior, who desires all men to be saved and to come to the knowledge of the truth. For there is one God and one Mediator between God and men, the Man Christ Jesus, who gave Himself a ransom for all.

The first thing God wants you to do is pray for those in authority. Do you know why He wants us to lead a "quiet and peaceable life in all godliness and reverence"? Unless a nation possesses peace and quiet, the gospel cannot be preached.

In times of governmental breakdown, war, and famine, the gospel by and large is no longer preached or proclaimed. But God desires that all men be saved.

Pray for quietness and peace. Pray for your government so all can come to this wonderful Mediator, the Lord Jesus, "who gave Himself a ransom for all."

Get A Global Vision

I think we, as Americans, are the most unthankful people since the children of Israel wandered in the wilderness. We have so much to be thankful for that we have no business griping about anything. Being godly is not enough; we must also be content: "Godliness with contentment is great gain" (1 Timothy 6:6).

Here is a verse you can pray:

> All the ends of the world shall remember and turn to the Lord, and all the families of the nations shall worship before You. For the kingdom is the Lord's, and He rules over the nations— Psalm 22:27-28.

When I read that, I got excited because it says "all the ends of the world" and includes the Middle East, Central America, the Soviet Union, Europe,

Canada, Beirut, Saudi Arabia—"*all* the ends of the world shall remember and turn to the Lord."

Therefore, you can pray, "Lord, You said in Your Word that all the families of the nations will worship You. I am asking that it happen for Beirut and the Moslems. I am asking that it happen for Nicaragua and the rebels. I am asking You to reveal Yourself. Lord, You said that Your Kingdom rules over all." In this way you can pray for world evangelism.

Then you can pray, "Lord, Your Word says that You rule over all the nations. I am asking You in Jesus' name to rule over Moscow, Washington, D.C., Beirut, Jerusalem, Paris, etc. The Kingdom belongs to You, God. You rule. So I am asking You to do what You, Yourself, wrote. I believe that what You said is true, and I am bringing it before Your throne."

The Bible tells us that God thwarts all the plans of the nations. The Kremlin can sit in Moscow and plan all day, but the Bible says,

> The Lord brings the counsel of the nations to nothing; He makes the plans of the people of no effect. The counsel of the Lord stands forever, the plans of His heart to all generations. Blessed is the nation whose God is the Lord, and the people whom He has chosen as His own inheritance—Psalm 33:10-12.

You can say to the Lord, "Bring the counsel of Arafat, Kadaffi, Khomeini, and Castro to nothing. Ruin their plans. Let the counsel of the Lord stand forever and the plan of Your heart be to all generations. Bless the people of Israel, whom You have chosen for Your own inheritance."

When we pray through a scripture like that, we will not have trouble believing because it is the Word of God. God is not in conflict with Himself, and these are His thoughts.

When we pray God's words, we will get God's answers. Therefore, the incense that rises up from our prayers is registered in heaven and will help control the destiny of the world's leaders.

Isaiah 40:15-17 gives another important perspective on God's relation to nations:

> Behold, the nations are as a drop in a bucket, and are counted as the small dust on the balance. . . . Lebanon is not sufficient to burn, nor its beasts sufficient for a burnt offering. All nations before Him are as nothing, and they are counted by Him less than nothing and worthless.

Stand In The Gap

When we pray for the nations, we often feel overwhelmed. I have heard good people say, "We had better not pray against the Prince of Persia or we will get in over our heads trying to bind such huge principalities."

Don't be afraid of principalities! A principality is no bigger than any other demon to Jesus. We must not pray in *our* name. But we can take on anything in *Jesus'* name. Any other attitude is fear and unbelief. The Bible says that all the nations are counted by God as "less than nothing and worthless."

What blocks prayer is our thinking that nations and leaders are big wheels while we are only grass-hoppers. We are sons of the Most High God! In the power of Jesus' name, we will affect the history of this planet—Moscow will not, and Washington will not. No human potentate will control history. We, the Church, will direct the course of events through intercession.

God looks at the nations and says, "They are a puny speck of water in a bucket. All of them together are as small dust."

You can pray, "Lord, You said the nations are as a drop in a bucket. Do You see what Syria has planned for Israel? Would You take Your little finger, God, and move Syria's influence off the scene?"

Before God, all nations are as nothing. It is the Church and the saints that are valuable to Him.

Isaiah 40:23 says that God "makes the judges of the earth useless." We think of the Supreme Court and are awed by their prestige and power. But their power comes by human decrees.

Such decrees have nothing to do with the will of God. They can say it is all right to murder babies, but that does not change the will of God. The Supreme Court cannot overrule the character of God. Although they wear fancy black robes, the Bible says that God makes the judges "useless."

Take that verse and pray for our Supreme Court. Pray that the Lord will bring those judges who stand against His purposes, holiness, and Scriptures to nothing.

Psalm 119:126 also concerns our Supreme Court: "It is time for thee, Lord, to work: for they have made void thy law" (*KJV*). I pray this verse often: "God, You said it's time for You to move, and I agree with You. Our Supreme Court has made void Your law. They have laughed, sneered, and mocked. They have said it is acceptable to murder babies. We cannot change them, God, but we ask You to move in accordance with Psalm 119:126."

Moving the Supreme Court is the key to the future of this republic. If we fail to change that court, this nation will be in real difficulty.

The prophet Isaiah says that, "[God] saw that there was no man, and wondered that there was no intercessor" (Isaiah 59:16). When God looks out of heaven today, He wonders that He cannot find an intercessor. When God looks down on your city, is He going to say, "I wonder why, with so many Christians alive, nobody will pray?"

God *needs* prayer in order to act. He does the acting, but we must do the asking. Can you say to God, "You are not going to wonder about America, because here am I; I will intercede, and I will pray"? You need to become an active part of a faithful intercessory group.

Prayer and intercession are two entirely different things: a prayer meeting is where you pray for yourself and your ingrown toenail; intercession is where you get into the very Spirit of God, become involved in His purposes, and pray in accordance with God Himself. You identify with Him and the person, situation, or nation for which you are praying. Pray with such pain and agony that you are caught up into the Spirit of God and the spirit of the nation or individual.

In closing, let me suggest 1 Chronicles 12:32 as a verse upon which to base your prayers for our leaders. Pray that they would be like the "children of Issachar who had understanding of the times, to know what Israel ought to do."

Pray, "Lord God, make our president, his staff, and his cabinet like the sons of Issachar. Let them have understanding of the times and what the United States should do."

As you learn to pray effectively for our nation and the world, you will help direct and influence people's lives. God is looking for faithful intercessors. Will you stand in the gap? Or will you wait for "someone else" to do it?

11

INTERCESSION AND THE DESTINY OF A NATION

The destiny of the United States of America is in our hands. I do not just mean the hands of the Church but those who know how to pray. The destiny of our nation is in the hands of the intercessors.

Ezekiel 22:23-31 is an involved passage concerning prophets, priests, princes, and people. With those four *Ps* in mind, let us read:

> And the word of the Lord came to me, saying, "Son of man, say to [Israel]: 'You are a land that is not cleansed or rained on in the day of indignation.'
>
> "The conspiracy of her *prophets* in her midst is like a roaring lion tearing the prey; they have devoured people; they have taken treasure and precious things; they have made many widows in her midst. Her *priests* have violated My law and profaned My holy things;

they have not distinguished between the holy and unholy, nor have they made known the difference between the unclean and the clean; and they have hidden their eyes from My Sabbaths, so that I am profaned among them. Her *princes* in her midst are like wolves tearing the prey, to shed blood, to destroy people, and to get dishonest gain. Her *prophets* plastered them with untempered mortar, seeing false visions, and divining lies for them, saying, 'Thus says the Lord God,' when the Lord had not spoken. The *people* of the land have used oppressions, committed robbery, and mistreated the poor and needy; and they wrongfully oppress the stranger.

"So I sought for a man among them who would make a wall, and stand in the gap before Me on behalf of the land, that I should not destroy it; but I found no one. Therefore I have poured out My indignation on them; I have consumed them with the fire of My wrath; and I have recompensed their deeds on their own heads," says the Lord God—*Italics added*.

Prophets are supposed to save and warn people from folly and impending doom. Any true prophet would save a family, a person, or a nation.

He would cry, "Get out of this sin or it will destroy you." This passage says these prophets are like roaring lions: they "tear the prey and devour the people." These "prophets" are in a reverse role.

Next the Lord says that the priests have violated His law, profaned His holy things, and failed to distinguish "between the holy and the unholy and the clean and the unclean." Sounds like America, doesn't it? Many Christians go to the same movies, watch the same TV shows, and read the same books that the world does. As God's people, we need to make a distinction between the holy and the profane. And we need godly pastors to help point the way.

After exposing the priests, God deals with the princes, stating that they are like wolves "tearing the prey, to shed blood, to destroy people, and to get dishonest gain." These princes (political leaders) couldn't be corrupt if the Church was doing its job. Instead of just shouting at the political system, we need to realize that before princes can get control of a nation, there have to be profane priests and devouring prophets. *The problem lies with the Church and its coldness.*

"Her prophets plastered them with untempered mortar, seeing false visions, and divining lies." When a person is living in sin, their message will be affected. I knew a man living in adultery, and he prophecied at almost every church service— and every prophecy concerned grace. I believe in grace, but when someone is living in sin, truth gets white-washed and plastered over. All he talks about is love and forgiveness.

Who Will Fill The Gap?

Describing a total breakdown of society, Ezekiel 22 speaks to prophets, priests, princes, and people. The people commit robbery, mistreat the poor and the needy, and oppress the stranger. And so they are condemned as greedy and uncaring.

Verse 30 gives us God's solution: "So I sought for a man among them who would make a wall, and stand in the gap before Me on behalf of the land that I should not destroy it; but I found no one." Please notice that it doesn't just say "stand in the gap" but "stand in the gap *before Me* on behalf of the land." That's intercession. And it just takes *one person.*

This reminds me of the story of the little boy who stuck his thumb in the dike and saved his city from devastation. America needs some men who will be intercessors—praying, standing in the gap, and filling up the breach in the wall.

Look at the last phrase of the 30th verse: "but I found *no one.*" Our number one sin is prayerlessness. This sin of omission is greater than sins of commission. Be that man who stands in the breach in the wall!

Verse 31 starts with the word "therefore": "Therefore I have poured out My indignation on them. . . ." In other words, either we intercede or we get judgment. God said that He consumed them with the fire of His wrath because no one was praying.

If we don't pray, we are going to get fire. There could even be nuclear judgment on our nation. I believe this is as relevant and serious a passage on intercession for America as any you can find.

But the Lord gives us great hope: "When the enemy comes in like a flood, the Spirit of the Lord will lift up a standard against him" (Isaiah 59:19).

The enemy *is* attacking our nation with a flood of wickedness, homosexuality, pornography, permissiveness, and humanism, and someone has to lift up a standard. Someone has to plug up the gap in the wall with intercession.

Look at the first verse of Isaiah 59: "Behold, the Lord's hand is not shortened, that it cannot save; nor His ear heavy, that it cannot hear."

Nothing is wrong with God. Prayer will work. God's hand is not disabled. The total responsibility for the condition of our country rests on the Church's shoulders. Nothing is wrong with God's willingness to answer prayer. The problem is that we preach and talk about prayer, but we don't pray.

Sharpen Your Sword

2 Chronicles 7:14 says that if we do *four* things, God will do *three* things:

"If my people who are called by My name will humble themselves, and pray and seek My face, and turn from their wicked ways, then I will hear from heaven, and will forgive their sin and heal their land."

If our country falls, it will not be the homosexual's fault. Alcoholics, dope-heads, and crack-users won't cause America's destruction. It isn't the sinners who must repent. God says, "If *My* people which are called by My name. . . ." The only ones who have to repent are God's people. Christians will be responsible if the United States falls.

This verse follows a deliberate progression. Humbling yourself is simply admitting, "I'm not what I could be; I'm not what I ought to be." To admit that you are lacking is not enough; you must pray consistently about your need. Yet, that is still not enough: "*Humble* themselves, and *pray* and *seek* My face."

Seeking God's face is different than just praying. It means having a personal relationship with Jesus—a face to face encounter with God—so you know what is on His heart. It means being such a close friend to God that you make sure you see His face every morning.

The steps to getting out of sin are humbling yourself, praying, and seeking His face. Then you can take the fourth step and *turn from your sin.*

That is how you get out of it. I know, experientially, that is true. God says that if we do those four things, He will hear from heaven, forgive our sins, and heal the United States of America.

Do you believe America needs healing? The destiny of our nation is in the intercessors' hands. You need to take hold of God's Word and apply it.

Hebrews 4:12 says, "The word of God is living and powerful, and sharper than any two-edged sword." When you pray a scripture, you are pulling the sword out of its sheath, swinging it in the heavenlies, and waging spiritual warfare.

The Word of God is a living, powerful, sharp sword. Its words must be unsheathed by prayer. We can affect the destiny of our children and our nation.

Remember, our warfare is not against flesh and blood. The weapons of our warfare are "not carnal, but mighty through God to the pulling down of strong holds" (2 Corinthians 10:4 *KJV*).

Building Godly Foundations

Our number one weapon is *prayer.* An army's success is no greater than its communication lines. Through prayer, we pull down the strongholds of the enemy, whether they are controlling the Supreme Court or the president.

The Bible contains some passages that can help us pray for our president, whoever he might be. Proverbs 21:1, for example, says, "The king's heart is in the hand of the Lord, like the rivers of water; He turns it wherever He wishes."

This scripture teaches that a king's heart is like a channel of a river, which God can change in whatever direction He chooses. Picture the huge gigantic hand of God with our president in the middle.

We can pray right now, "God, we put our president in Your hand. We want him, his staff, his cabinet, and both houses of Congress to be in Your hand. Lord, turn their hearts, like a river, wherever You want to direct them—in Jesus' name." Pray this for any authority—your king, husband, father, pastor, governor, or president.

Proverbs 25:5 talks about a leader's staff workers: "Take away the wicked from before the king, and his throne will be established in righteousness." Did you know that the president doesn't run a nation, but his staff does? Who are the wicked before the "king" in the present administration? I don't have the slightest idea. Only God knows: "Lord, we pray that You remove whomever You consider as the wicked around our president. Take them away from before him so his throne may be established in righteousness. In Jesus' name."

We just took our sword out and went to work on the executive staff, severing some of them from influence over the president. The Bible is a sword that is unsheathed by prayer.

What about the president's integrity? Proverbs 16:12 says, "It is an abomination for kings to commit wickedness, for a throne is established by righteousness." "Lord, we pray that our president will not commit wickedness but will do what is right. Help him to love Your people rather than the influential jet set. Please establish his throne on righteousness."

Besides providing scriptures we can pray for our leaders, the Bible also contains many passages that concern nations. Following are a few verses to pray for the United States.

"Blessed is the nation whose God is the Lord" (Psalm 33:12).

"The wicked shall be turned into hell, and all the nations that forget God" (Psalm 9:17 *KJV*).

"Lord, we want to confess before Your throne that You are the Lord of the United States of America. We *want* You to be Lord, and we want to be Yours. We don't forget You, and we don't want to be turned into the hell of a nuclear fire. In Jesus' name, Amen."

"If the foundations are destroyed, what can the righteous do?" (Psalm 11:3). For example, the Supreme Court says it is illegal to display the Ten Commandments in a school room. If you take away the foundations (the Ten Commandments, the Sermon on the Mount, basic moral integrity), the whole building will collapse. We need to pray that our country will begin rebuilding the godly ideals upon which it was founded.

Psalm 12:8 says, "The wicked strut about on every side, when vileness [or wickedness] is exalted among the sons of men" (*NASB*). In America, the wicked and the homosexuals hold parades, strut up and down, and brag about being perverts. They break all laws of decency, do what is against nature, and enjoy having reprobate minds. This sounds very much like the Roman Empire, doesn't it? (See Romans 1.) Truly, sin is "a reproach to any people." (See Proverbs 14:34.)

If you traveled to other countries, Kenya, for example, you would see America's X-rated films advertised on movie marquees. Kenyans think that Christians in America commit adultery continuously. If you go to Israel, their favorite telecast is *Dallas.* The picture portrayed of America gives the strong impression that all we do is jump in and out of bed with somebody else's husband or wife. They do not respect us.

Even the communists sneer and laugh. They say, "Don't come with your Western ethics and destroy the morality of Russia." The Moslems say, "We don't want to be a degenerate society like the Christian West." If I were God, I'd have trouble deciding which country to judge because the communist nations have less divorce, alcoholism, pornography, and immorality than we do!

Sin is a reproach. Hang your head in shame as an American when you are overseas, because many people believe we are a wicked, degenerate society. Hollywood movies and American television give a bad impression of the West.

An excellent verse to pray for the nation is, ''He rules by His might forever; His eyes keep watch on the nations; let not the rebellious exalt themselves'' (Psalm 66:7 *NASB*). What a tremendous prayer request—that the rebellious not be allowed to exalt themselves.

The destiny of our nation is in the intercessors' hands, and it is prayer time. At this writing, I do not believe that America will be destroyed because I believe that you and I are going to intercede. Through intercession, we can turn America's ethics around.

In summary, God told Ezekiel that the prophets (preachers) are dishonest; the truth is all plastered over; the priests (teachers) don't even know what is holy or unholy; the people are greedy; and the princes (politicians) are wolves. But God said that He would relent if He could find a man to stand in the gap.

I believe that a man or a woman will be found who will intercede. Someone will put their finger in the dike, and there will be revival and restoration of holiness and righteousness. Our only options are a revival of intercession or the certainty of judgment.

12

PRAYING FOR PER-SONAL HOLINESS

How does sin hinder prayer? How does holiness relate to our prayer life? Sometimes we don't realize how many factors enter into effective prayer, but they always drive us back to God. As we study this, we will read through some negative verses, which force us to be realistic, and some positive verses, which give us hope. Think of a car battery's negative and positive terminals—both are necessary for the car to run.

The Lord has much to say about His reaction to prayer. Consider these verses from Proverbs:

> The sacrifice of the wicked is an abomination to the Lord, but the prayer of the upright is His delight. . . . The Lord is far from the wicked, but He hears the prayer of the righteous. . . . One who turns away his ear from hearing the law, even his prayer shall be an abomination—Proverbs 15:8,29; 28:9.

It would be hard to find a more dramatic word than "abomination." If I told God I was going to turn my ear away from what the Scripture says, then He would say, "Okay, Ernie, your prayer is an abomination to Me."

We often tend to pray for "they," "them," "she," or "he." But the problem is not with our pastor, our brother, or our sister—it is with us. The Lord desires us to be quiet and listen to what He says about how we pray.

Jeremiah 14:10-12 talks about those who wander:

> Thus says the Lord to this people: "Thus they have loved to wander; they have not restrained their feet. Therefore the Lord does not accept them; He will remember their iniquity now, and pun- ish their sins." Then the Lord said to me, "Do not pray for this people, for their good. When they fast, I will not hear their cry; and when they offer burnt offering and grain offering, I will not accept them. But I will consume them by the sword, by the famine, and by the pestilence."

Here Jeremiah is told *not* to pray for Israel.

Some may say, "That is the Old Testament." Then let's consider a passage from the New Testament:

He who would love life and see good days, let him refrain his tongue from evil, and his lips from speaking guile; let him turn away from evil and do good; let him seek peace and pursue it. For the eyes of the Lord are on the righteous, and His ears are open to their prayers; but the face of the Lord is against those who do evil—1 Peter 3:10-12.

Whether we like to admit it or not, it is possible to reach the position where God's face is against us.

Heed God's Warning

If we can receive a warning, it will take us to the place of repentance and prayer. 1 John 5:16-17 is a warning:

If anyone sees his brother sinning a sin which does not lead to death, he will ask, and He will give him life for those who commit sin not leading to death. There is sin leading to death. I do not say that he should pray about that. All unrighteousness is sin, and there is sin not leading to death.

There is a sin leading to death, and we are not to pray about this. What is sin that leads to death?

Is it blasphemy of the Holy Spirit? Is it adultery? Is it stealing from church finances? Is it breaking one of the Ten Commandments?

Whenever a person persists in any state of willful disobedience, *any* of those sins can be a sin causing God to bring his life to an end.

A popular preacher once traveled across the country, committing adultery from town to town. He developed cancer and died in two months. No one could have prayed him back to health because he was sinning a sin unto death. Another famous preacher began to drink. A prophet of God told him to repent of the alcoholism or the Lord would remove him. He refused to repent, had a car accident, and died. There is sin unto death.

Many of us get on our knees and say, "Oh, God, what is wrong with You? Why aren't You answering my prayer?" We fail to look at these verses that deal with the consequences of sin. They are not positive, and all we want to hear is fluff.

I am not saying that everyone who dies is sinning, but there is a sin unto death because the Bible talks about it. Sometimes the Lord would say, "It's just like Jeremiah—you can pray all you want, but I am going to remove them because they are a reproach to My name and the Church."

The apostle John writes,

> For if our heart condemns us, God is greater than our heart, and knows all things. Beloved, if our heart does not

condemn us, we have confidence toward God. And whatever we ask we receive from Him, because we keep His commandments and do those things that are pleasing in His sight. And this is His commandment: that we should believe on the name of His Son Jesus Christ and love one another, as He gave us commandment—1 John 3:20-23.

We receive answers because we are obedient and pleasing to the Lord Jesus Christ. Does your heart condemn you? If so, the Scripture says that God is greater than your heart. If my heart is condemning me over the way I lived this week, God is greater than my heart—if *I* am condemning myself, what is *God* thinking?

We need to understand God's view on holiness in regard to prayer. If you aren't holy, *that's where to start with your prayers.*

If I regard iniquity in my heart, the Lord will not hear. But certainly God has heard me; He has attended to the voice of my prayer. Blessed be God, who has not turned away my prayer, nor His mercy from me!—Psalm 66:18-20.

That is positive. First, the eighteenth verse talks about reality: Is iniquity in my heart? If someone has a sin habit, disregarding that habit is the opposite of repenting. Whatever it is, we must say, "If I regard iniquity in my heart, the Lord will not hear my prayer."

Most people forget to read the nineteenth verse—the positive part: "But certainly God has heard me; He has attended to my prayer. Blessed be God, who has not turned away my prayer."

If you are messing around with sin, you need to have a good repentance meeting. You need to get flat on your face and stay there until you can say, "Nothing in my heart condemns me."

Honesty With God

Many times we blame God for unanswered prayer when we aren't right with Him—we aren't honest. Instead we play games. Face reality—we need to be holy when we come into the presence of the Lord. Have you sinned? If so, the way to enter back into holiness is honest, two-way prayer.

"When you come to appear before Me, who has required this from your hand, to trample my courts? Bring no more futile sacrifices; incense is an abomination to Me. The New Moons, the Sabbaths, the calling assemblies—I cannot endure iniquity and the sacred meeting. Your New Moons and your appointed feasts My soul hates; they are a trouble to Me, I am weary of bearing them. . . . Even though you make many prayers, I will not hear. Your hands are full of blood"—Isaiah 1:12-15.

This situation is similar to the one in Jeremiah. God says He does not like our solemn assemblies, and He will hide when you pray. Yet, He gives the solution in Isaiah 1:16-20:

"Wash yourselves, make yourselves clean; put away the evil of your doings from before My eyes. Cease to do evil, learn to do good; seek justice, reprove the oppressor; defend the fatherless, plead for the widow. Come now, and let us reason together," says the Lord, "though your sins are like scarlet, they shall be as white as snow; though they are red like crimson, they shall be as wool. If you are willing and obedient, you shall eat the good of the land; but if you refuse and rebel, you shall be devoured by the sword"; for the mouth of the Lord has spoken.

We will learn to "do good" during our quiet time as we study the Word. "Come now, let us reason together," is *written to the person who is not getting their prayers answered*. The children of Israel had messed up and displeased God, and God's reply was, "Let us reason."

Have you ever knelt and said, "Lord, what's wrong in my life? What should I change?" Psalm 139:23-24 says: "Search me, Oh God . . . and see if there is any wicked way in me."

What is reasoning with the Lord? You must get down on your knees and say, "Lord, does anything in my life displease you?" The Holy Spirit may put in your mind a time when you were rude, selfish, or angry. God wants to answer your prayers, and you must deal with your negative areas so He can.

We usually apply these verses to non-Christians, but we need to apply them to ourselves. The Lord says there is forgiveness for us. Before we enter true intercession, we must step away from the "they" and "them" attitude, examine ourselves, and make sure we are honest with God.

If we refuse to be obedient, we will be "devoured by the sword." The sword of the Holy Spirit is the Word of God, and the Scripture devours those who go against it. I would rather line up with the Word than have the Word become a sword against me.

God wants us to come to Him with our petitions and confessions:

> "I, even I, am He who blots out your transgressions for My own sake; and I will not remember your sins. Put Me in remembrance; let us contend together; state your case, that you may be acquitted"—Isaiah 43:25-26.

You can say, "I state my case. Jesus died for my sins, and the Lord says in His Word that He will not remember my sins. He will blot them out for His own name's sake."

When you pray, the devil will tell you that you're not worthy. And your answer to him is, "That's right. That's why I'm praying." Satan will tell you that you are a sinner. And your answer should be, "Why do you think I'm praying?" The only way to get out of that sin and defeat is to pray.

Look at the power in this passage:

> "I have blotted out, like a thick cloud, your transgressions, and like a cloud, your sins. *Return to Me, for I have redeemed you.*" Sing, O heavens, for the Lord has done it! . . . For the Lord has redeemed Jacob, and glorified Himself in Israel—Isaiah 44:22-23, *Italics added*.

Have you ever felt that there was a cloud between you and God? Well, there is—but not because God left. He's just as close to you as He ever was. Look at His Word. He says He's blotted out your sins. Return to Him, for He has redeemed you.

Be honest with the Lord; ask Him to remove the cloud between you and Him. If you are lukewarm and carnal, with one foot in the devil's kingdom, you are half backslidden. In this condition you have no prayer power. You couldn't. You must start with yourself. These verses give you hope, and they are realistic. Every time you disobey, it's as if a cloud comes down on you. When that cloud is removed, singing starts again.

This is more than forgiveness as we know it. For your sin to be blotted out means that it does not exist any more. It's *gone.* God does not remember it. You may have had an abortion, committed adultery, or done any number of things. Yet God completely blots it out and forgives you. Isn't that exciting?

Living In The Light

Christians must face the fact that holiness is essential to prayer. Unrighteousness blocks prayer power. We must start with ourselves and make sure we are honest.

> If we walk in the light as He is in the light, we have fellowship with one another, and the blood of Jesus Christ His Son cleanses us from all sin—1 John 1:7.

This is the purpose of this chapter. Make sure that you are walking in the light and living in fellowship with God. Either you are or you aren't. If you are not, the good news is that Jesus' blood will cleanse you from all sin. The condition is that you step back into the light. You must be sincere.

If you compare how much a mom and dad love their child, Jesus loves you a trillion times more. He ascended to the prayer office for you, and His prayers are always answered.

Picture Jesus sitting at the right hand of God. Meditate for ten or fifteen seconds. It will help your faith. Jesus loves you and is delighted with you. Ask for forgiveness if that is what you need. If you bad habits, ask Him to help you eliminate them from your life. Focus your prayer on Jesus.

Go to a quiet place, stop talking, and listen. Realize that you are bringing your prayer request before the very Son of God, who has already died, won the victory, and passed through the heavens. He sits at the right hand of God the Father. The highest person in heaven is your best friend and Savior. Jesus wants you to live a holy life more than you want to live it.

13

AVOIDING SELFISH PRAYERS

One of the best known and most often quoted stories in the Bible is the parable of the Prodigal Son. (See Luke 15:11-32.) Jesus tells of the irresponsible young man who demanded his inheritance and squandered all the money in riotous living. Finally, so destitute that he would "gladly have filled his stomach with the pods that the swine ate" (verse 16), the wayward son humbled himself and returned home to beg forgiveness and a servant's place in his father's household.

But he was greeted by a loving, merciful father, who brought out "the best robe and put it on him, and put a ring on his hand and sandals on his feet" (verse 22). Then his father commanded that the fatted calf be killed, and everyone "began to be merry" (verse 24).

When the prodigal son returned home, he received the *best robe* his father had. As believers, the best robe we can ever receive is the robe of righteousness—the robe of salvation. When a person comes to Jesus Christ, the Lord takes a perfect robe from the heavenly closet—without spot or stain—wraps the believer in it, declares him righteous, and looks at him as if he had never sinned. God looks down from heaven and says, "You are perfect because I clothe you in My own righteousness!"

The believer is shocked that God runs down the road, embraces him, kisses him, loves him, and adorns him in righteousness. When the believer protests that he is not worthy, the Lord responds, "I know you are not worthy. Nevertheless, I am going to give you My signet ring."

In New Testament times, each person had a private drawing made into a signet ring that was pressed into clay tablets to leave a seal as a signature or authorization. The ring in the Prodigal Son story suggests that all the authority belonging to a believer is given back to him at repentance. God says, "Even though you have strayed and wandered, now that you are home, I give you My authority to witness, testify, preach, and pray—authority to use My name and get an answer from heaven."

When the astounded believer responds, "A robe of righteousness and a ring?" the Lord adds, "I also have a new pair of shoes for you—the gospel of peace—so that your feet will be beautiful. You will go up and down the mountains of people's problems—their divorces, their drug and alcohol addictions, and their impure minds and mouths. You will run up to these people and say, 'I have good news! Jesus can set you free.' "

The most wonderful thing about a backslider's return home is that his joy is restored. Don't we serve a wonderful God? We expect a rebuke. But our Father says, "I think we'll have a party. Kill the fatted calf, and we will make merry." We can laugh again, shout again, worship again, and smile again, even though we have been in the pigpen of sin.

Give-me-itis

For years, I overlooked an interesting principle in this parable. While the story tells us of God's wonderful grace upon the son's return, it also gives us some insight into the prodigal's fall. Note verses twelve and nineteen. In essence, verse twelve tells us that the son says, "Father, I want my inheritance. *I want* my portion. Give me, give me, *give me.*" After straying, wasting his money in harlotry, and becoming a slave—after slopping hogs and wishing *he* had as much to eat as the hogs—the son now cries, "I am no longer worthy to be called your son. *Make me* like one of your hired servants."

We can practice two kinds of prayer: the "give-me's" and the "make-me's." The reason we backslide is that we get the "give-me's." Selfish prayer can cause us to drift from God. "Give me money.

Give me status. Give me a new house, a new car, and new furniture. Give me a husband. Give me prosperity, popularity, favor. I want my inheritance. What's wrong with God? Why aren't my prayers being answered?"

Give me is "the spirit" of the prodigal. The first step in his backsliding is that his prayers are completely selfish. He's contracted *give-me-itis*. That is a dangerous disease.

But when God gets through with him, the prodigal says, "*Make me* a man of God." Do you see the difference?

For us, the prayer should be, "Make me holy. Make me a blessing. Make me a friend to someone who is lonely. Make me generous. Make me a person of integrity. I want to be *made* something instead of just receiving something."

You can make your own list, but you can begin to see that the person who prays for God to make him something is entirely different from someone who has give-me-itis. Instead of saying, "Give me a good wife," maybe you should say, "Make me a good husband." Instead of saying, "Give me good teenagers," maybe you should say, "Make me a good father." Instead of saying, "Give me good parents," maybe you should say, "Make me so obedient that my parents say, 'We have a great kid.'"

In a recent letter from Reverent David Chu in Hong Kong, one of the missionaries our church supports, he made a statement that both challenged and frightened me:

"Recently we have been reminded that one billion young people will pass through the critical ages of thirteen and twenty-three by the year 2,000. One billion young people on the move. They will rarely listen to lectures. We cannot stop them. Their power is unavoidable. One billion human lives, each with his or her own unique hopes and visions, fears and hurts. We cannot afford to ignore a single one of these complex, precious persons. Still less can we ignore one billion.

"Today they live in a world we have made; tomorrow they will make the world in which we live. Today they are asking questions; tomorrow they will dictate answers. Today they look for a leader; tomorrow they must become leaders. Today they are searching for direction; tomorrow they must provide it. And if we do not win their hearts today, they will break our hearts tomorrow."

Young people are looking for leaders. I believe every person in every age group is looking for leadership. People enjoy and expect leadership. That is why I feel good when I stand up and say I am against beer, whiskey, and wine. We may lose a few people (although we probably would have lost them anyway because they were kissing the world), but the strong ones say, "Hey, there *is* righteous leadership! There *are* strong pastors and elders. There *is* a strong church."

"Today they look for leaders; tomorrow they must become leaders." When I read that statement, I thought, Who wants to get on the "give-me" side and ask for appliances? Does that statement inspire you to say, "God, make me an excellent parent; help me take a strong stand for righteousness"?

Embracing The World

Consider James 4:1-3:

> Where do wars and fights come from among you? Do they not come from your desires for pleasure that war in your members? You lust and do not have. You murder and covet and cannot obtain. You fight and war. Yet you do not have because you do not ask. You ask and you do not receive, because you ask amiss, that you may spend it on your pleasures.

Many people ask for things selfishly. They want their prayers answered for pleasure. They want the give-me list. God says, "No!"

The hedonist asks, "What's wrong with You, God? You won't answer my prayers!"
The Bible says,

> Adulterers and adulteresses! Do you not know that friendship with the world is enmity with God? Whoever therefore wants to be a friend of the world makes himself an enemy of God—James 4:4.

Are you embracing the world's standards? If you cling to promiscuity, immorality, masturbation, and all the X-rated, filthy stuff perpetrated in the world and then ask, "Why aren't my prayers answered?" God will respond, "You are an adulterer—the world's friend—and you have become My enemy."

Perhaps you had better pray that you will be a man or woman of God. Maybe you should ask God to make you pure and holy: "Lord, make me a blessing to someone; make me usable."

You are never too young, too old, or too anything to be a blessing. The prodigal son became a blessing the moment he arrived home. And as soon as you get back in the Spirit, whether you are fifteen or seventy-five, you can be a blessing.

Psalm 106:13-15 says,

> They soon forgot His works; they did not wait for His counsel, but lusted exceedingly in the wilderness, and

tested God in the desert. And He gave
them their request, but sent leanness
into their soul.

This scripture proves that we can talk God into
answering a prayer that is not best for us. They
were screaming for quail, and God said, "I'll give
you quail." If you read the context in the Old Testament (Numbers 11), you will find that quail was
practically coming out of their nostrils.

They forgot God's works and refused to wait
for His counsel. Instead of asking, "God, how
should I pray?" they said, "Here I am to name and
claim, God. You had better be my Santa Claus, or
I won't serve You. You may think You are God,
but I'm going to tell You what You are going to
give me—and how soon and how much."

That is blasphemy! You will never make God
your errand boy or talk Him into fulfilling your
lust. You may get some quail—He gave the Israelites their request, but He also sent leanness.

The Effects Of Selfishness

We've been talking about prayer that moves
away from selfishness and motivates God to make
us what He wants. Two Old Testament examples
illustrate the nature and effects of *give-me-itis*.

Genesis chapters thirty and thirty-one tell the
story of Jacob's flight from his father-in-law, Laban.
Jacob took his possessions, gathered his family,

and left for his homeland. Rachel, his wife, secretly took the household gods from her father's house and hid them in her saddlebags. Furious, Laban pursued Jacob and demanded the household idols from him. Unaware of Rachel's sin, Jacob allowed Laban to search the entire group.

Rachel succeeded in hiding the idols, but her "give-me" actions helped to widen the rift between her husband and her father. Her selfishness also led to more sin, since she was forced to lie to her father and continue her hold on idols abhorrent to God.

Ironically, Jacob, with his mouth, confessed Rachel's death. He had said, "With whomever you find your gods, do not let him live" (Genesis 31:32). A few chapters later, Rachel gave birth to Benjamin, and Jacob's words came true—she died giving birth. The curse he had pronounced came on the person he loved most—his Rachel.

Another example of the devastating effects of selfishness is found in Joshua 7. After defeating Jericho, Joshua took his army against the city of Ai. This time, however, Joshua's army was defeated, and "The hearts of the people melted and became like water" (Joshua 7:5).

When Joshua fell before the Lord and cried out for an answer, the Lord said,

> "Get up! Why do you lie thus on your face? Israel has sinned, and they have also transgressed My covenant which I

commanded them. For they have even taken some of the accursed things, and have both stolen and deceived; and they have also put it among their own stuff. Therefore the children of Israel could not stand before their enemies, but turned their backs before their enemies, because they have become doomed to destruction. Neither will I be with you anymore, unless you destroy the accursed from among you''—Joshua 7:10-12.

Joshua soon discovered that Achan, of the tribe of Judah, had stolen from Jerico a "beautiful Babylonian garment, two hundred shekels of silver, and a wedge of gold weighing fifty shekels" (Joshua 7:21). He had hidden the spoils in his tent in defiance of God's command that nothing be taken from Jericho. Because of his sin, he and his family were stoned to death and cremated.

The consequences of Achan's "give-me" actions were serious on several levels. He turned God against the entire nation and caused the defeat of the army and the deaths of many men. He jeopardized the success of Israel, for God said, "Neither will I be with you anymore, unless you destroy the accursed from among you." Finally, he brought destruction on his entire family. His greedy attitude was destructive from beginning to end.

Give-me-itis always creates problems and fosters sin. Ultimately, it hinders prayer and brings about disaster.

Do you have anything hidden in your saddlebags? Do you have anything hidden in the center of your heart? If you want to pray, pray until nothing hidden remains in your heart—articles or attitudes. You may disagree with how I defined worldliness earlier, so look at your own definition. What does today's Christian look like when he is wearing a Babylonian garment? What is it that makes us of Babylon—the world system?

Achan couldn't keep his hands off that wedge of gold. Money was on the top of his "give-me" list. He got it, hid it, and thought he was safe. He thought no one knew. *But God knew!* Achan needed to do some praying, not for a wedge of gold or for worldliness but to be a man of God.

If there is something hidden in your life that you would not want me or your best Christian friend to know about, to that extent you are a hypocrite. If you have a filthy VHS tape, pornography, or anything you would be ashamed to reveal publicly, you need to get off your camel and open your saddlebag. Destroy *that thing*. It may be a bad attitude, hate, or bitterness. It could be anything.

You need to pray until you are a Nathanael. When Jesus saw Nathanael, He said, "Behold, an Israelite indeed, in whom is no guile!" (John 1:47). "No guile" means no deceit, cunningness, craftiness, or double-heartedness.

Pray until you can say, "As far as I know, I do not hate anybody or harbor any secret sin. Nothing is hidden in my tent. I have destroyed every Babylonian garment."

The prodigal son says, "Give me my inheritance. I want it now." The repentant son says, "Make me holy." Selfish prayers cause people to leave the Father's house. Prayers for holiness cause people to be holy.

I have a challenge for you: be like that repentant prodigal son. Whatever your pigpen is—hate, pornography, selfish prayers, or anything else—why not leave it? Come to the end of yourself, and run home to Daddy. That is something to pray about!

Pray with all your heart until you are back home wearing the robe, the ring, and the sandals, with joy in your heart. God is waiting. He is not angry with you. You can come home.

14

THE VALUE OF A PRAYER LANGUAGE

During my early years as a preacher, I knew the Bible spoke about tongues, and I knew they were real. Never foolish enough to say tongues were of the devil, I felt similar to many people today: "Why do I need it? Will it do me any good?" We should be able to give a sound, scriptural, thought-out answer to that question.

When we say tongues, we're talking about the Holy Spirit speaking through us a language that we've never learned—it can be angelic or human.

On the day of Pentecost, about fourteen language groups were present when the Holy Spirit fell, and the apostles preached the gospel in languages they never learned. (See Acts 2:1-13.) But preaching is not the only purpose for tongues. If we read on in Acts, we find an entirely different situation at Cornelius' house.

> While Peter was still speaking these words, the Holy Spirit fell upon all those

who heard the word. And those of the circumcision who believed were astonished, as many as came with Peter, because the gift of the Holy Spirit had been poured out on the Gentiles also. For they heard them speak with tongues and magnify God—Acts 10:44-46.

In this passage, it wasn't the preacher who was speaking in tongues but the congregation, who all had received salvation. These were Cornelius' friends, which probably means they were of the same language group. In verse forty-six, they were "magnifying God" in tongues. The gift of tongues, in this case, was used for praise and worship.

Talking To God

For he who speaks in a tongue does not speak to men but to God, for no one understands him; however, in the spirit he speaks mysteries—1 Corinthians 14:2.

Tongues is more than preaching or talking to men. It's a way to communicate with God, which makes it invaluable.

Satan cannot understand tongues, either. If we are speaking in a human language, he can understand it. But the only way the devil could understand an angelic tongue would be if God gave Satan the interpretation. He's not about to do that, and 1 Corinthians 14:2 substantiates this.

Many years ago, a Roman Catholic priest, Robert L. Smith, spoke to our congregation. We had dinner together before the meeting, and since all of us had received the Baptism of the Holy Spirit, I suggested that we thank God in tongues for our food.

As we lifted our hands and began to bless the Lord in tongues, I saw that Rev. Smith had a look of surprise on his face. When we finished praying, he said, "I understood every word you said. I received my seminary training in Japan and lived there eight years. You were speaking perfect Japanese!"

After the meal, we prayed for the upcoming service. As we knelt and began to pray in the Spirit, the Lord again let my prayer be in Japanese. The Reverend quoted back the Japanese phrases and explained them.

He said, "What you prayed in Japanese was, 'O God lift us up into Your prayer hut, into the heavenly places, and let us praise Your holy name tonight in the service!' The strange thing is that you prayed classical Japanese, which foreigners can't speak. Western people cannot pronounce it correctly because the sounds are too different. But you sounded like a native Japanese person!"

This happened again at church when we prayed for people. One of our elders had a pain similar to a heart attack (numb on his left side), and I placed my hand on his shoulder and prayed for him. Rev. Smith's eyes opened wide, and he quoted back the Japanese for me: "Lord, heal his heart on the inside and the outside." By this time I was getting uncomfortable because he knew what I was saying, and I didn't. But I trusted the Lord.

Next, we began to pray for a lady. As I prayed in tongues, I looked over to Rev. Smith, and he was grinning. I said a few more phrases and quit. Then he said, "Do you know what you said? A Japanese idiom meaning, 'that's right on, that's really it, or that's what I want!' When you saw that I understood what you were saying, you used that idiom, saying, 'Well, anyway, God, that's what I want.' " This experience testifies to the validity of tongues in the present day.

Paul says in 1 Corinthians 13:1,

> Though I speak with the tongues of men and of angels, but have not love, I have become as sounding brass or a clanging cymbal.

This verse infers that we can move in the gifts of the Spirit yet be out of order and out of the love of God. We can pray in tongues anytime we choose to, but if we were to jump up in the middle of a service and interrupt the preacher, we would be out of order. The tongue would still be real, but our exercising of it would be from our own will and would be unkind and rude.

The same is true of the other gifts. Suppose I discerned that a person had a spirit of seduction, and I announced it to everybody. That would not manifest the love of God.

In 1 Corinthians 13:1-3, Paul mentions five gifts of the Holy Spirit. He mentions tongues, prophecy, the word of wisdom, understanding mysteries (word of knowledge), and the gift of faith. He uses the word "all" for emphasis: " . . . understanding *all* mysteries and *all* knowledge, and though I have *all* faith, so that I could remove mountains, but have not love, I am nothing" (*Italics added*).

How would you like to have your life add up to zero on Judgment Day? The love of God has to motivate everything we do if we want our lives to amount to something.

Worship And Intercession

A popular misconception says the Bible teaches that tongues is the least of the gifts. The Bible does not say that anywhere. The gifts are not necessarily listed in order of importance. (See 1 Corinthians 12:28.) Being the last on the list does not reflect the value of the gift. In 1 Corinthians 13:13, "And now abide faith, hope, love," love is listed last, but it certainly isn't least.

Spiritual gifts are like tools. For example, there are several different types of saws. Which is best, the buzz saw, skill saw, keyhole saw, or chain saw? That depends upon the need. If you're going to cut down a tree, you don't want a keyhole saw. If you're going to put a light fixture in the ceiling, you don't want a chain saw. The need determines which tool is best.

If somebody has a demon, discernment of spirits is best. For someone who is sick, the gift of healing is best. If someone needs direction for their life, the word of wisdom is best. But if we want to worship God, the gift of tongues is best. It's an insult to God to say that worship is least. To God, worship and praise are somewhere on top of the list because the Bible says, "The Father is seeking such to worship Him" (John 4:23).

Besides praise and worship, the gift of tongues is used for prayer. Look at 1 Corinthians 14:14: "If I pray in a tongue, my spirit prays, but my understanding is unfruitful." The verb in this verse is not "speak" but "pray." Most people misquote this verse.

We are created in the image of God, and, like God, we are three-fold beings—body, mind, and spirit. When we pray in tongues, it's not our mind praying but our spirit. Until we receive the Baptism in the Holy Spirit and pray in tongues, the deepest part of us, our spirit, has never fully praised God.

Psychology is based on the presupposition that the mind is the center of a person. But the Bible says we have something deeper than our intellect—the spirit.

It's easy to identify with this because all of us have been hurt in our spirit at one time or another. Someone acted like they loved us and then stabbed us in the back. The wound goes deeper than our mind; it goes into our spirit.

Isaiah prophesied that the Messiah would come to heal the brokenhearted and those with a "spirit" of heaviness. (See Isaiah 61.) In other words, Jesus came to heal us deep in our spirit and "set at liberty them that are bruised" (Luke 4:18 *KJV*). He's talking about the bruises on our spirit.

We send our children to school to train their intellects at age five, producing a civilization directed and governed by minds. Then someone comes along and says, "You can pray with something deeper than your brain—you've got a spirit."

Some of us find that very hard to accept. Yet, how much praise can we think of with our minds? I don't think anyone can come up with more than fifteen or twenty phrases: "I love You, Jesus; I worship You; I adore You; bless the Lord; and so on." If we will enter into the Spirit and praise Him in tongues, we won't have to go through our limited mental capacity.

Jesus said of the believer, "Out of his heart will flow rivers of living water" (John 7:38). The *Amplified* version translates "heart" *innermost being*. The Holy Spirit unites with our human spirit, creating a river of worship or intercession that flows out of us.

Most of us know God from our chin up. With the Baptism in the Holy Spirit, our spirit is *released* to worship God fully.

One Step At A Time

"Whom will he teach knowledge? And whom will he make to understand the message? Those just weaned from milk? Those just drawn from the breasts? For precept must be upon precept, precept upon precept, line upon line, line upon line, here a little, there a little"— Isaiah 28:9-10.

Little babies need to be weaned from the bottle. Many Christians hear salvation sermons for forty or fifty years. There comes a time to move past the infant stage.

That's how I received the Baptism, and that's exactly how others will receive it. They'll come across a verse in John and say, "I wonder if he could be right?" Then they'll come across another verse, maybe in Isaiah. At a service or a Bible study they'll hear a little. It begins to stack up—line upon line, scripture upon scripture—until one day they're convinced. All we have to do is keep preaching the truth and loving people.

In *The Cross And The Switchblade*, David Wilkerson said, "To have complete victory over dope you have to get the Baptism." Soon after that

I read, *They Speak With Other Tongues*. At first, I didn't receive what that book had to say. Then I came across a verse here and another one there. One night I found myself alone with God, and the truth of the Baptism of the Holy Spirit unfolded for me. It's a step by step, gradual growing process.

Paul quoted the next two verses of that passage from Isaiah while talking about tongues in First Corinthians 14:21:

> For with stammering lips and another tongue He will speak to this people, to whom He said, "This is the rest with which you may cause the weary to rest," and "This is the refreshing"; yet they would not hear—Isaiah 28:11-12.

While praying with a brother in Nebraska several years ago, I noticed he was stammering. I said, "Wait a minute, relax. The Holy Spirit is a Spirit of peace and gentleness."

Have you ever heard a 33 speed record played at 78? I explained that this was exactly what he sounded like and asked him to sit down, lift his hands, and tell Jesus how much he loved Him. After that, he immediately began to praise Jesus in a beautiful, quiet, fluent tongue. He had stammering lips at first because he was fighting God as a result of his emotionalism.

What does "this" in verse twelve refer to? God is telling us that speaking in tongues is what will bring rest and refreshing to the weary. "Yet they would not hear." Many people don't want to hear it. How then can tongues be their *rest?*

When we pray in tongues, the Holy Spirit flows into our spirit, along with His fruit—peace, joy, strength, and faith. We are immediately put at rest.

Shortly after receiving the Baptism, I came away from a particular service very discouraged. While taking a walk later that day, Satan attacked me: "Full of the Holy Spirit—Ha! You're just making up those tongues! How could you preach a sermon that poor if you were full of the Holy Spirit? The best thing for you to do is resign."

Determining not to listen to Satan, I began to pray in tongues. I walked a block or two, and suddenly, like a shift in gears, God gave me a brand new language. I wasn't emotional, just obedient to what the Word said.

At the service that night I had free utterance and liberty. The Word flowed out, and God gave me revelation. Scriptures seemed to jump off the page at me, and the Lord showed me things faster than I could speak them.

At home, I asked the Lord, "Why was I tongue-tied in the morning, when in the evening I had liberty, freedom, power, revelation, and anointing? What made the difference?" The Lord answered, "Because you prayed in tongues, you edified yourself; you got so full that you overflowed. Never preach again without tongues as part of your sermon preparation."

I had been out of the Lord's rest, and I was weary. Ministering all day leaves a person drained spiritually. Many of you have experienced that. After praying in tongues, I felt refreshed.

Building Up Faith

Before receiving the Baptism in the Holy Spirit, I thought speaking in tongues was selfish because it edifies yourself. (See 1 Corinthians 14:4.) But it is not selfish to edify or build ourselves up in the inner man. If someone were to ask us to pray for their little boy, it would be tragic to say, "Call back tomorrow because I'm not full of God right now."

We need to be full of God all the time. If we're not built up, then we're run down. Would we rather be run down—needing someone to build us up— or built up, so *we* can edify the one who's run down? We need to be full to overflowing so we can be a blessing to other people.

With tongues, we can pray without ceasing—while driving or doing the dishes. When I get into tight situations, I pray in tongues immediately. I know that if I pray in tongues the Holy Spirit will clear the air. My spirit and the Holy Spirit will line up and flow together.

The Lord has shown me three keys to tight situations: 1) Be quiet; 2) Pray in tongues; 3) Don't speak until God does.

One time a brother got extremely upset with me over some little point. I shifted into tongues silently and waited for direction from the Lord on how and what to speak. The brother continued talking, not really listening for answers. When he finished, God spoke to me, and I said, "You know what brother? I love you." He was astonished. It didn't make any difference whether I had all the answers to his questions. What he needed to know was that I loved him.

Praying in tongues will benefit our relationships with our spouse, children, and people we meet in daily life. The fruit of the Holy Spirit will flow through us if we will be quiet, pray in tongues, and keep silent until God speaks.

When we pray in tongues, we build ourselves up in faith. Jude 20-21 says,

> But you, beloved, building yourselves
> up on your most holy faith, praying in
> the Holy Spirit, keep yourselves in the
> love of God, looking for the mercy of
> our Lord Jesus Christ unto eternal life.

I have literally felt faith grow in me while praying in tongues.

Everyone wants more faith. We can increase our faith in two ways—"Hearing . . . the Word of God" (Romans 10:17). And "praying in the Spirit" (Jude 20-21). When we are in the Spirit, He flows into us. The Holy Spirit is called the "spirit of faith" in 2 Corinthians 4:13. As we pray in tongues, we can proceed from doubt and questioning to assurance and answers.

Jude also tells us to "keep yourselves in the love of God." While I was pulling out of a Sears parking lot, a man almost smashed his car into mine. I began to gripe and murmur. Suddenly feeling the love of God, I turned to my wife, Dee, and asked her if she was praying in tongues. She said, "How did you know?" I felt the love of God and couldn't stay mad. When we are tempted to get bitter, we'll place ourselves in the love of God if we move into the Spirit and begin to pray in tongues.

The Divine Intercessor

Whenever the Bible uses the phrase, "praying in the spirit," it is talking about the Spirit within us praying. The Holy Spirit intercedes for us, helping us when we don't know what to pray:

> Likewise the Spirit also helps in our weaknesses. For we do not know what we should pray for as we ought, but the Spirit Himself makes intercession for us with groanings which cannot be uttered. Now He who searches the hearts knows what the mind of the Spirit is, because He makes intercession for the saints according to the will of God—Romans 8:26-27.

The Holy Spirit knows what to pray for in each situation. How much do we understand about somebody else's needs or spiritual problems? To be able to let the Holy Spirit intercede through us is a tremendous advantage.

A woman in our church was drying her dishes one morning when the Spirit of God came upon her. She began praying in tongues in an entirely different language than her usual prayer language. She felt such a strong urge to pray that she left the kitchen, knelt down, and travailed in prayer for fifteen or twenty minutes. The new language was so strange that she asked the Lord what it was. The Lord told her the language was Swahili, an African tongue. Deeply impressed by the intense intercession, she wrote down the time it occurred.

About three weeks later, a Christian family she knew told her about a missionary to Africa they were both acquainted with. The missionary had been flown to Miami with serious breast cancer. Comparing dates and consulting time differences between Africa and America, they figured out that at the exact hour the missionary was being put on the plane in critical condition, the Spirit impressed our sister in Kansas City to pray. Do you know what happened? That missionary was healed and returned to Africa!

We are told to pray "in the spirit, being watchful . . . for all the saints" (Ephesians 6:18). As we intercede, we must watch for what God will show us.

While praying in tongues, sometimes we'll see mental pictures of people. This is how we receive discernment of spirits, words of wisdom, and words of knowledge. We find out what's going on through this tool of the Holy Spirit. *Tongues is the gateway to operating and moving in the other gifts of the Spirit.* We are in the flow of God, and He can show us what He is doing.

One morning while I was praying in tongues, a mental picture of one of the the teenagers in our church came to me. She was wearing a beautiful red dress. A neighbor girl walked up to her and joked about the Baptism of the Holy Spirit and tongues. The girl from our church laughed along with her. When she did, a rip showed up in her red dress. She sewed it up, but I could still see the shape of the rip.

I asked the Lord what it meant. He said, "That beautiful dress represents her witness. When she laughed along at the things of God, she rent her testimony. Although she sewed it up, that will always affect her witness to her neighbor."

That evening, I went over to this teenager's house to talk to her. I told her what I saw and asked her if this had happened or was going to happen. Tears began to run down her cheeks. The night before, exactly what God showed me had happened. She felt very sorry about it. Evidently, this incident offended the Holy Spirit so deeply that He wanted her to repent and ask Jesus to forgive her, which she did.

Tongues is a supernatural way to pray for people—for salvation or deliverance. The Holy Spirit needs somebody to intercede through. He needs someone to pray and battle in heavenly places. When we intercede in tongues, we're coming against all the powers of Satan and breaking down strongholds. Pray in tongues constantly.

Moving In The Supernatural

Jesus Christ and the disciples were right in their method of evangelism. The Lord reached people through the gift of healing. That was His plan. Churches have substituted programs for gifts. What people are hungry for is not words about God but the power of God. The key to ministry is Jesus Christ, but the key to His might and His power is prayer.

The best kind of prayer is not with our puny brains but with the Spirit. When we pray in tongues, the Spirit comes for healing, preaching, understanding, and revelation. Tongues is one of the keys to the Christian life. It's the difference between going somewhere on a scooter and going somewhere in a Cadillac. The gifts of the Holy Spirit are God's tools, and they get evangelism done.

There are three kinds of people: believers who are Spirit-filled, believers who occupy the room of the uninformed, and lost people. Many people are saved, and they know Jesus. But when it comes to the deep things and the gifts of God, they occupy the place of the uninformed: "If you bless with the spirit, how will he who occupies the place of the uninformed say 'Amen'?" (1 Corinthians 14:16).

Bless those that curse you, using supernatural prayer to impart the blessing. We need to be informed and let the Holy Spirit bless people through us.

Paul is often misquoted as saying that he would rather speak five words with his understanding than ten thousand words in an unknown tongue. Paul did not say that. He said,

> I thank my God I speak with tongues more than you all; *yet in the church* I would rather speak five words with my understanding, that I may teach others also, than ten thousand words in a tongue—1 Corinthians 14:18-19, *Italics added*.

If Paul spoke in tongues more than all the Corinthians, he must have done an awful lot of tongue talking. Tongues help us receive personal instruction in our private devotions. God has given me tongues and interpretations for myself at home while praying alone. He has told me what to do and confirmed it by prophecy.

> Therefore tongues are for a sign, not
> to those who believe but to unbelievers;
> but prophesying is not for unbelievers
> but for those who believe. But if all
> prophesy, and an unbeliever or an unin-
> formed person comes in, he is con-
> vinced by all—1 Corinthians 14:22,24.

This passage, which can be confusing, is not talking about believing in salvation. It is talking about believing in the Baptism of the Holy Spirit. Tongues are a sign for those who do not believe in the Baptism of the Holy Spirit. This may be an entirely different way of looking at the passage than you're used to, but Paul is speaking to Christians because he has just mentioned those who occupy the room of the uninformed.

Everyone who receives the Baptism in the Holy Spirit receives the gift of tongues. Although some people have never spoken in tongues, the gift lies dormant inside them. They received the gift of tongues when they prayed for the Baptism in the Holy Spirit; they just didn't exercise it.

> "These signs will follow those who
> believe: In My name they will cast out
> demons; they will speak with new
> tongues; they will take up serpents; and
> if they drink anything deadly, it will by
> no means hurt them"—Mark 16:17-18.

The context of this passage is the Great Commission: "Go into all the world and preach the gospel" (verse 15) . . . "And these signs will follow."

The day I received the Baptism of the Holy Spirit, Jesus spoke to me as I put the key in the ignition of my car. "Neglect not the gift that is within thee." Until then I had spoken only a few syllables, but immediately I began to pray those syllables. Then the dam burst, and that language poured out of me. As I was driving west on I-70, God said to me, "Pray that you may interpret." He gave me this interpretation while I was praying in the unknown tongue: "This is the day of salvation for Gary." At the time, I pastored a small Baptist church, and the only person in the congregation named Gary was a teenager.

I drove straight to Gary's house. His dad asked why I had come, and I replied that I wanted to talk to Gary. The young man had just arrived home from school, so his dad directed me into Gary's room. He, too, asked why I had come. Although I did not tell him how I received prophecy, I looked him right in the eye and said, "Gary, today is the day of salvation for you." Tears flowed, and he was instantly on his knees praying to receive Jesus.

After my talk with Gary, I went to Bethany Hospital in Kansas City. In an elevator, I met a lady and her husband. As the elevator began to move, the Lord said to me, "Pray for that woman."

Inside, I responded that I had never prayed with anybody for their healing. The Lord replied, "Obey me." With that, I introduced myself and asked if I might pray for her. She and her husband both agreed to let me pray, so I laid my hands on her head. Suddenly, strange syllables came out of me. When the elevator door opened, tears were running off the woman's cheeks, and she said, "I felt power like electricity go all through my body. I know I am healed."

Many people who are filled with the Holy Spirit have not used their prayer language. It is in them, but it is dormant. A person can have the Baptism in the Holy Spirit and never pray in tongues.

Communicating With Headquarters

Christians are funny sometimes. We talk about putting on "the whole armor of God" (Ephesians 6:11), yet we stop in the middle of the passage we are quoting. The apostle Paul exhorts us to "take the helmet of salvation, and the sword of the Spirit, which is the word of God; *praying always with all prayer and supplication in the spirit*" (Ephesians 6:17-18, *Italics added*). What good is wearing armor if we have lost communication? Any army, whether armed with tanks, jets, or rockets, is defeated if it cannot communicate with the commander.

The most important action for the army of God is communicating with the Commander in Chief.

He has given us a supernatural way of staying in communication. Do you stay in communication by praying in the Spirit?

The gift of tongues is clearly much more than the initial physical evidence of the Baptism of the Holy Spirit. If we will worship God in tongues every day, then the Spirit will flow in us, and we will be full all over again. If we don't pray in tongues daily, we're missing the point. The gift of praying in tongues is the supernatural means of staying Spirit-filled.

15

CORPORATE INTERCES-SORY PRAYER GROUPS

Corporate intercession is a power tool of the Christian. From the word "corporate" we get the word "corporation," meaning a group of people in unity for one purpose. Corporate prayer, therefore, happens when a group of people unite for the purpose of intercession.

1 Corinthians 14:40 says, "Let all things be done decently and in order." That applies to prayer meetings. Since prayer meetings sometimes get a little "wild-n-woolly," I want to begin by focusing on the practical aspects of corporate prayer.

Do's And Don'ts Of Intercession

Corporate prayer is not a time to hang out your dirty laundry. Neither is it a gossip session, slander session, speculation session, or suspicion session. Corporate prayer is for *intercession*.

When interceding avoid grunts, mechanical noises, groans, and other weird sounds. Do not put on a "King James" or any strange, unnatural voice. Avoid artificial tones, whines, and gusto authority. These are all *learned responses* and do not contribute to intercession. Instead, these satanic or soulish interruptions succeed in stopping intercession. An old locomotive steam engine can use its steam to blow its horn or move the train down the track. We need to do more than toot.

Have you ever feared taking a visitor to church because "Brother Smith" will have one of his fits? All the way to church you pray, "God, I love Brother Smith, but bind him from getting weird today. Visitors have enough trouble understanding our raising hands, clapping, and looking happy in church." Just being joyful in church is shock enough for most visitors.

We were in a prayer meeting one night, and one man in the crowd exhibited great gusto authority. You could see it coming. His breathing got heavier, and all of a sudden he let out a "prophetic prayer" so loud I couldn't tell if it was addressed to God or for God. Screaming at the top of his lungs, he gave the impression that authority is measured in decibels. God was nowhere in it. We need to grow up and pray sensibly.

Always bring your Bible to a prayer meeting and read only the *relevant verses* in a chapter. At one prayer meeting, somebody read an entire chapter of sixty-three verses. During the Beirut hostage crisis, I prayed Psalm 91:11-12 for the hostages. My wife, Dee, and I had been praying and reading the

Bible together. When I read those verses about angels, the Spirit spoke to my heart. I knew the key was angelic help, so I prayed those two scriptures . The Lord will speak to your heart and show you what verses to pray for specific situations.

When you pray, either pray quietly enough so that no one hears you or loudly enough so that everyone hears you. Nothing is more frustrating than someone speaking into their hands or toward the floor. Not everyone hears as sharply as you do. Have you ever been in a prayer meeting where you could only catch every fifth word? You don't know whether to say "Amen" or not.

Don't be afraid of silence in a prayer meeting:

> Do not be rash with your mouth, and
> let not your heart utter anything hastily
> before God. For God is in heaven, and
> you on earth; therefore let your words
> be few—Ecclesiastes 5:2.

In the Sermon on the Mount, Jesus said, "They think that they shall be heard for their much speaking" (Matthew 6:7 *KJV*). Remember, He said to avoid vain repetitions. Instead of shopping-list prayers, long repetitious prayers, and world-tour prayers, pray in tongues softly until something comes into your spirit from heaven to pray. Stay with the same topic until it is thoroughly prayed out and the Holy Spirit gives peace to proceed. Never abruptly change subjects.

Do not use prayer to grind a private ax. During the Jesus People movement, a certain lady was frustrated with men who had long hair. At every Saturday night prayer meeting she talked about it in her prayers. Each week it intensified, until it finally came out as a prophecy on Sunday morning: "Yea, saith God, cut your hair!" That is grinding a private ax. In our prayers, we must be sensitive to the Holy Spirit's guidance about the true need in each situation.

Never pray *horizontally*. We aren't praying to teach or inform others who are present. Have you ever heard, "Oh, God, You know what You have been showing me. You know what You spoke to me last Tuesday morning. . . ." What we are doing is trying to teach the group what God revealed to us. This is praying horizontally instead of vertically. Along the same line, avoid preaching and expounding Bible outlines. *God does not need to hear sermons*.

Concentrate on the person presently praying rather than what you are going to pray next. Agree with that person's prayer if you have a witness from the Holy Spirit; otherwise, do not say "Amen" to it. Once during a prayer meeting, someone prayed a prayer that would have shut down the economy of every nation in the world if it had been answered. Instead of saying "Amen" to it, I said in my heart, "Oh God, don't answer that, in the name of Jesus." Sometimes you can't agree with what people pray.

Sensitivity To The Spirit

The anointing of the Holy Spirit must never be poured on someone's fleshly prayer. We must know what to do when someone's prayer is not of the Holy Spirit. Exodus 30:30-32 deals with prayer because it talks about the anointing oil put on the priest:

> "And you shall anoint Aaron and his sons, and sanctify them, that they may minister to Me as priests. And you shall speak to the children of Israel, saying: 'This shall be a holy anointing oil to Me throughout your generations. It shall not be poured on man's flesh.' "

A priest is an intercessor—someone who takes another's problem or circumstance and presents it to the Lord. The Bible teaches that we Christians are all believer-priests. (See 1 Peter 2:5,9.) When we pray, we want to come under *God's* anointing.

At the same time, never be so arrogant as to judge or criticize another person's prayer. They are allowing you to listen to a sacred moment. If they are hurting, pray for them rather than criticize their prayers.

I was meeting with a group of people whom I love when someone started praying. I sat there judging and criticizing. God rebuked me. He said,

"That man's talking to Me, and you're privileged to listen. Don't you ever criticize another man while he's talking to Me." I began to pray for that brother.

When somebody prays in a foolish or unwise way, they are most likely going through sorrow, pain, tribulations, and trials. Their emotionalism may even be a manifestation of their trouble. Everyone in that prayer meeting should instantly be praying for the person who is hurting or out of line. This way, instead of losing your prayer meeting to judgment and criticism, suddenly the hurting person becomes (silently, to be sure) the focus of everybody else's prayers. I think this is a very sweet way to deal with a serious problem.

Everyone who has been in a prayer meeting has probably made the mistake of criticizing. We need to be extremely sensitive to the Holy Spirit and watchful in our prayers.

Acts 4:23-31 is the only account of a prayer meeting—what they prayed, how they prayed—in the Book of Acts. Because of that, it is a good passage on which to meditate. The Sanhedrin had said in 4:17, "Speak to no man in this name." In the following verse they "commanded them not to speak at all nor teach in the name of Jesus." Then in verse twenty-one the Sanhedrin threatened them with many threats. They warned against witnessing, preaching, public meetings, and mentioning the name of Jesus.

The apostles' response was to meet for prayer. First they found two verses to claim from the Old Testament. The first verse was Psalm 146:6, which says that God is the Creator and Lord of all things. They said, "God, You're in control. You can handle this situation." Then they claimed and prayed Psalm 2:2-3: "Why did the nations rage . . . The kings of the earth took their stand, and the rulers were gathered together against the Lord and against His Christ" (Acts 4:25-26). They said, in effect, "The kings, Herod and Pilate, have raised up against Your Anointed, Jesus."

Seeing that these verses fit their situation, the apostles prayed through them. But they only took hold of a couple of specific verses from a chapter.

Next, the apostles asked for two petitions. Instead of saying, "Let's get out of this terrible mess," they asked for boldness to go through it. Secondly, they requested signs, wonders, and miracles to confound the Sanhedrin.

These men of God received ten answers to prayer in this one chapter. First, "The place where they assembled was shaken"—literally, like an earthquake (verse 31). In other words, that is the *manifest presence of God*. God's presence is everywhere, whether you feel it or not; the manifest presence is when you can feel it or see it.

Second, God refilled them with the Holy Spirit. Some people need to be refilled with the Holy Spirit because they leaked! One way to get refilled is to become part of a corporate prayer meeting.

Third, they "spoke the word of God with boldness" (verse 31).

Fourth, they had compassion and love for each other.

Fifth, they shared everything and experienced total unselfishness. Communism says, "What you have is mine." Christianity says, "What I have is yours."

Sixth, they were of one heart and soul.

Seventh, they had great power.

Eighth, they preached the message of Jesus' resurrection with power.

Ninth, they gave alms. Everyone who had a need was satisfied.

Tenth, they sold everything, gathered the money, and laid it at the apostles' feet. In other words, they conquered materialism. That was a powerful prayer meeting!

Many home groups spend about half the time praying—I mean really praying for each others' children and other very real situations. Everyone needs to be in some type of corporate prayer meeting. You are kidding yourself if you think you are on fire for God when all you do is pray over your meals or on your way to work.

Take Hold Of God

The purpose of this chapter is not to teach you about prayer but to get you into a corporate prayer meeting. There are many different ways: home groups, Wednesday nights at church, at work, or with your family. Some people meet during their lunch hour and pray. Corporate prayer is where you really do business with God.

Satan is a supernatural enemy with supernatural intelligence and power. We must not presume that we can get together and utter a few petitions or shouts and have the whole front line of hell collapse. I couldn't be more serious. Satan has supernatural plans for your children, your wife, your marriage, and your finances. No wonder we have such tremendous family problems in this society. Few people today take prayer seriously.

> We are all like an unclean thing, and all our righteousnesses are like filthy rags; we all fade as a leaf, and our iniquities, like the wind, have taken us away. And there is no one who calls on Your name, who stirs himself up to take hold of You—Isaiah 64:6-7.

Many of us are familiar with the sixth verse but totally unfamiliar with the seventh. God wants us to stir ourselves up and take hold of Him. He wants us to call on His name.

Apply Colossians 2:18-19 to the subject of corporate prayer:

> Let no one defraud you of your reward, taking delight in false humility

and worship of angels, intruding into those things which he has not seen, vainly puffed up by his fleshly mind, and not holding fast to the Head, from whom all the body, nourished and knit together by joints and ligaments, grows with the increase which is from God.

First of all, don't let anyone rob you of your reward or prize. Many of us are defrauded because we do not pray. Many times we pray from our fleshly mind. Sometimes we intrude into areas without forethought because we do not hold fast to the Head. Much in this verse can be applied to prayer. Growth is from God. Any growth not from God is cancer, and believers can have spiritual cancer.

The gift of the word of knowledge is the key to getting direction for how the group should pray. Authority is important in a corporate prayer meeting. The *leader* of an intercessory prayer group should be responsible for having a word of knowledge or discerning a word given by a member of the group.

During a plague of snakes (Numbers 21), the Lord told Moses to get a brass snake and put it on a pole. Whoever looked at it would live. That was a word of knowledge. In the natural, that was about the stupidest thing Moses could have done. Where did he get such an idea to put a brass snake on a pole? In the Bible, brass always refers to judgment. A brass snake means the snake judged. He said, "Look and live." (See verse 8.) This is a type of Christ in the New Testament because on the cross the serpent (Satan) was judged. And whoever looks at Jesus lives. *Look and live.*

A person leading a prayer meeting needs to be able to hear God's voice or at least discern the words that come. Any group without a leader has a vacuum, and Satan will fill it. There must be leadership.

Lay Down Your Life

Intercession is far more than personal prayer and petition, such as for your ingrown toenail or Aunt Sadie's earache. It involves your whole being— spirit, soul, and body. When we care enough about people going to hell, our spirit, soul, and everything in us wants to be a soul winner.

> He that goeth forth and weepeth, bearing precious seed, shall doubtless come again with rejoicing, bringing his sheaves with him—Psalm 126:6 *KJV.*

To intercede effectively, you must lay down your life again and again. That includes your *schedule.* You will never obey this message without choosing to lay down some of your time. Satan is afraid of prayer, and he will see to it that you have every excuse *not* to commit yourself to a prayer meeting. Intercession requires a deeper level of commitment than prayer. It is a group of prayer warriors getting with and sticking to the program.

Intercession involves identification with the plans, the ways, and the very character and being of God. When Daniel began to pray (Daniel 9), he saw God's plan, purpose, and prophecy, and he concentrated his total being on that. In Daniel chapter ten he received an answer, but it was only after he, himself, became involved with the very purpose of God.

True intercession also involves identification with the person, situation, or nation for which you are praying. Twice when God was going to destroy the whole nation of Israel, Moses fell on his face in intercession. He so identified with and loved his people that he said, "God, blot my name out of your book, but don't wipe out Israel." (See Exodus 32:32.) And God heard him. Every Israelite would have been struck dead except that Moses stood in between judgment and the people. This is more than prayer—this is intercession.

Another example of intercession occurs in Genesis chapter eighteen. Abraham's nephew lived in the homosexual cities of Sodom and Gomorrah. Angels told Abraham they were going to destroy those cities. He identified with an individual—his nephew—and called out to God.

Abraham said, in effect, "Will not the judge of the whole earth do right? It isn't fair to judge everybody because the group is failing. God, You can't do that." He said, "Wouldn't you save the city if there were fifty, . . . forty, . . ." until he gradually narrowed it down to ten.

When fire and brimstone fell from heaven, the only reason Lot wasn't killed was because somebody did more than pray.

Can you identify with your own son? Can you weep for your own daughters that are backslidden? Can you cry for your best friend from high school who is now a drug addict? Our lack of intercession convicts us and shows our *carnality*.

Being an intercessor involves being "after" the spirit instead of "after" the flesh. Romans 8:5 says, "They that are after the flesh do mind the things of the flesh; but they that are after the Spirit the things of the Spirit" (*KJV*). We cannot live to watch television and be an intercessor.

Intercession involves living an abiding life and being a *living sacrifice*. It involves being in union with God in a specific situation until you identify with His purposes and Spirit, travailing with inaudible words in the supernatural prayer language. Intercession involves making prayer the nucleus of your life instead of a peripheral function.

Will You Do It?

I want to challenge you today to join a corporate prayer group. We need to be part of a regularly scheduled meeting, interceding for our nation, our local church, our leaders, and our children.

And we need an outpouring of the Holy Spirit. Prayer should be so important that we will attend the meeting even if we have to miss something else.

God is challenging you today to move from prayer to corporate intercession. The intercessors are going to control the destiny of individuals and nations. But you can only be an intercessor when you agree to meet consistently at a specific time with a specific group.

Each intercessory group should have a particular focus. My anointing is to pray for the nations. I often center my prayers on, and get excited about, praying for America, the Supreme Court, and the president and his staff. I love to pray for those issues.

You may never get excited about praying for global crises or national affairs, but I know you can get excited about praying for your children. Once when our church was singing "His Name Is As An Ointment," I thought of my daughter, Renee, living thousands of miles away in Israel. It didn't take this father a second time through the chorus to begin to say, "Jesus, let Your healing and anointing fall on Renee. Your name, Jesus, Your flow, Your life, Your healing be upon my daughter."

We need to become intercessors, not merely pray-ers. The Holy Spirit is saying, "It's corporate prayer time—move into it, fathers, mothers, and leaders." Make this chapter a seed, not a sermon.

Do you want to be an intercessor instead of someone who prays once in a while? Are you willing to be an intercessor? Then pray this prayer:

"My God, come by Your sovereign grace and anoint me not merely to talk about prayer but to pray. Make me an intercessor, Lord. Give me grace, Lord, to make the sacrifice of time and the commitment to go regularly to a specific prayer meeting. Show me whom to pray for and with whom to pray. Make intercession central in my life.

"Forgive me, Lord, for the sin of prayerlessness and for not being identified with You and Your purposes. Forgive me for neglecting those who are hurting. Lord, I believe now that I am receiving a divine infusion of grace to pray. My mouth confession is: I am an intercessor. You have birthed in me grace to intercede. In Jesus name. Amen!"

16

HOW TO WATCH IN PRAYER

The subject of "watch and pray" frequently occurs in the Bible. In my research, I found thirty-one verses on this subject. Studying some of these scriptures will help you become an intercessor.

Proverbs 8:34-35 says,

> Blessed is the man who listens to me,
> watching daily at my gates, waiting at
> the posts of my doors. For whoever
> finds me finds life, and obtains favor
> from the Lord.

This scripture shows the importance of a daily appointment with God. You cannot watch and pray if you don't go before the throne of God every day. If you meet God four days out of seven, that means three days you are on your own. Thinking that you can survive with a quickie prayer on the way to work is dangerous. Too many Christians try to walk in their own strength.

In Bible times, the chief elders met to transact business at the city gates; they didn't have a courthouse. This verse is saying, "I want you to meet Me at the courthouse of heaven every day." The person who doesn't meet God daily is a sleeper instead of a watcher:

> I wait for the Lord, my soul waits, and in His word I do hope. My soul waits for the Lord more than those who watch for the morning—I say, more than those who watch for the morning—Psalm 130:5-6.

The psalmist waits for the Lord more than the guard on night duty waits for the morning. That is a long wait. The night guard waits for the sun with great longing—also with a strong conviction of the need to keep his post covered.

This is the personality type we need to have—type W. The "W" stands for watching and waiting for the Lord. This is even better than secular society's discussion of personality types "A" versus "B." We need to go to God daily, wait to hear what He wants us to do, and do it. Watching includes daily waiting.

Protection Through Prayer

The Lord Jesus talks about prayer and our families in Matthew 24:42-44:

"Watch therefore, for you do not know what hour your Lord is coming. But know this, that if the master of the house had known what hour the thief would come, he would have watched and not allowed his house to be broken into. Therefore you also be ready, for the Son of Man is coming at an hour when you do not expect Him."

We must watch so Satan doesn't get hold of our daughters or sons. Many children are backslidden in this modern television age because moms and dads do not pray for their sons and daughters. Satan breaks in, steals, kills, and destroys. Television totally desensitizes a family to the danger and power of sin.

The apostle Paul says, "Watch, stand fast in the faith, be brave, be strong" (1 Corinthians 16:13). The *King James Version* says, "Be men." Hey, men! How many of you would like to be a real man rather than a whimp? Then pray for your family. The hardest, most difficult, most important work you can do is to pray.

"Be diligent to know the state of your flocks, and attend to your herds" (Proverbs 27:23). In the margin of a good reference Bible it will literally say "face": "Be diligent to know the face of your flocks." Watching involves looking at people's faces. Anybody who is unable to look at his teenager and know whether they're in the Spirit or not is asleep. The glory of God is hard to miss, and when His glory is missing, it's obvious. You all have your little flock—your family—and you need to know each individual face.

Look at the countenance of your wife, husband, father, mother, pastor, or home group leader. Is there discouragement in their faces? Is a twinkle in their eye and a smile on their faces? Is the joy and anointing of the Holy Spirit there? The enemy likes to come, shut off prayer, and close our eyes. And while we sleep the sleep of death, Satan steals.

The concluding sentence of the parable of the foolish virgins and the wise virgins is, "Watch therefore, for you know neither the day nor the hour in which the Son of Man is coming" (Matthew 25:13). This passage is warning us to avoid ending up in the dark, as the foolish virgins did.

Is your candle lit? Letting your candle go out is the same as saying, "I used to pray, witness, and have a quiet time. I *used* to love going to church." Flicker, flicker, flicker? The winds of this age are blowing. If we find ourselves in a "used to" situation, it's time to watch! It's time to relight our candle and keep our lamp full of oil.

In the garden of Gethsemane Jesus spoke to His disciples:

"My soul is exceedingly sorrowful,
even to death. Stay here and watch with

Me." He went a little farther and fell on His face, and prayed, saying, "O My Father, if it is possible, let this cup pass from Me; nevertheless, not as I will, but as You will." Then He came to the disciples and found them asleep, and said to Peter, "What, could you not watch with Me one hour? Watch and pray, lest you enter into temptation. The spirit indeed is willing, but the flesh is weak"—Matthew 26:38-41.

The disciples didn't watch, and they did enter into temptation. Three times in the garden of Gethsemane Jesus told His disciples to watch and pray.

Nothing could be more accurate than that instruction of the Head of the Church to us: "Watch and pray, lest you enter into temptation." Keep your eyes wide open. Look out for Satan. Check your heart, and check your motives. Watch!

Take Time For Jesus

If your mouth confession and your heart confession is that Jesus is your Lord, yet you don't have time for Him, you are being hypocritical. Do you have an hour for the newspaper or for television? Do you have an hour for Jesus?

If you can't set aside an hour for God, can you give Him fifteen minutes? Gradually make it twenty minutes, a half hour, then bring it up to an hour. Do something every day. Never take a vacation from God. If you're too busy for God, you're too busy.

I used to think Martin Luther exaggerated when he said, "When I have an extremely busy day, I get up and spend an extra hour in prayer." My life was so far removed from such a commitment that I couldn't conceive it as possible.

The busier you are, the more necessary it is for you to pray. In fact, if you have that time alone with God, you will get twice as much done. This is true for studying, administrating, making phone calls, organizing, or doing housework. Things go better with *prayer!* It is a delight, not a tedious burden or duty.

We seldom notice that Paul finishes his discussion of the armor of God in the sixth chapter of Ephesians by encouraging prayer. Verse eighteen exhorts us to pray "always with all prayer and supplication in the Spirit, being watchful to this end with all perseverance and supplication for all the saints." Praying how often? "Always." With what? "Perseverance and supplication in the Spirit." And how attentive should our prayer be? "Watchful."

It won't do an army any good to have tanks, missiles, or airplanes if they have lost communication with their commander. The key to any army is communication. Weapons have to be triggered, and armor has to be mobilized.

Prayer is our last and most important piece of armor. It provides communication with our Commander in Chief and gives us direction. Prayer mobilizes.

Watch and pray so that you can escape the tribulation period:

> "But take heed to yourselves, lest your hearts be weighed down with carousing, drunkenness, and cares of this life, and that Day come on you unexpectedly. For it will come as a snare on all those who dwell on the face of the whole earth. Watch therefore, and pray always that you may be counted worthy [strong enough] to escape all these things that will come to pass, and to stand before the Son of Man"—Luke 21:34-36.

Everyone says the teaching of a rapture is escapism, but who is teaching "an escape"? Jesus is teaching escape. Who escapes? Those who watch and pray:

> "Take heed, watch and pray; for you do not know when the time is. It is like a man going to a far country, who left his house and gave authority to his servants, and to each his work, and commanded the doorkeeper to watch. Watch therefore, for you do not know when

the master of the house is coming—in the evening, at midnight, at the crowing of the rooster, or in the morning—lest, coming suddenly, he find you sleeping. And what I say to you, I say to all: Watch!''—Mark 13:33-37.

Four times in that one paragraph Jesus says to watch. He says we don't know when He is coming.

Regardless of whether a person believes in a pre, mid, or post-tribulation rapture, the issue is watching, not dating when it will occur. If you are asleep in sin, it won't make any difference when it happens.

In the book of Luke, we see a special blessing on those who are found watching when He comes:

> ''Let your waist be girded and your lamps burning; and you yourselves be like men who wait for their master, when he will return. . . . Blessed are those servants whom the master, when he comes, will find watching. Assuredly, I say to you that he will gird himself and have them sit down to eat, and will come and serve them''—Luke 12:35-37.

That is beyond comprehension. The King of kings wants to serve us! Doesn't that give you the determination to set aside a specific time to spend with Him, daily?

Be Faithful To The End

Some morning you may wake up and find the newspaper saying: "WORLD PEACE AT LAST! We've signed Salt Six. There'll be no more nuclear war." That will be the most important day in your entire life to pray:

> When they say, "Peace and safety!" then sudden destruction comes upon them, as labor pains upon a pregnant woman. And they shall not escape. But you brethren . . . *watch and be sober.* For God did not appoint us to wrath, but to obtain salvation through our Lord Jesus—1 Thessalonians 5:3-9, *Italics added.*

We must watch the world situation. There will be no peace until the Prince of Peace comes. 1 Peter 4:7 says that the "end of all things is at hand; therefore be serious and watchful in your prayers." If the end of all things is at hand, then we *have* to be serious about watching and praying.

Many people fall into temptation because they forget to watch and pray. We overcome temptation by being watchful:

> Be sober, be *vigilant;* because your adversary the devil walks about like a roaring lion, seeking whom he may

devour. Resist him, steadfast in the faith, knowing that the *same sufferings are experienced by your brotherhood* in the world—1 Peter 5:8-9, *Italics added*.

Satan tries to possess our future and depress us into wrong paths. I have been under satanic attack that almost resulted in my resigning from the pastorate. I seriously considered it for two years. Why? Because the devil tried to discourage and destroy me so he could possess my future.

Now I have victory over that. At first I didn't understand the satanic attack; but, after getting beat up round after round, I realized what Satan was trying to do.

I have talked with other pastors and Christian leaders across the country who have experienced a similar attack. There is a pattern in this: Satan steals and crushes our joy; then he can possess our vision. He tries to depress us so he can capture our future. Then he tries to get us to resign.

Why am I being this transparent? Because we all face the same afflictions and sufferings. I know that if the shepherds become discouraged and beat down, Satan can work the same demonic attack on you. He will try to crush your joy and steal the life blood out of your vision. Watch and pray! My trial was no different than yours. It wasn't any worse or any easier. It had the same kind of satanic pattern to it.

Pastors and church leaders, watch and pray for your flock. "Be watchful in all things, endure afflictions, do the work of an evangelist, fulfill your ministry" (2 Timothy 4:5).

Watch out for the wolf—the person who tries to draw the flock away from the true gospel:

> "Take heed to yourselves and to all the flock. . . . For I know this, that after my departure savage wolves will come in among you, not sparing the flock. Also from among yourselves men will rise up, speaking perverse things, to draw away the disciples after themselves. Therefore watch, and remember that for three years I did not cease to warn everyone night and day with tears"—Acts 20:28-31.

The Christian leader is responsible to *watch out* for the souls of the flock as one who must give an account. (See Hebrews 13:17.)

By the same token, you must watch and pray for your pastor and those in leadership:

> Continue earnestly in prayer, being vigilant [watchful] in it with thanksgiving; meanwhile praying also for [pastors, elders, deacons, home group leaders, Sunday School teachers] that God would

open to [them] a door for the word, to speak the mystery of Christ—Colossians 4:2-3.

Pray that doors would open to further the gospel. We need to watch out for and build each other up in intercession.

Jesus exhorts us to "be watchful, and strengthen the things which remain, that are ready to die" (Revelation 3:2). This is a *last days* verse for us who live in the period when Jesus said, "And because lawlessness is increased, most people's love will grow cold. But the one who endures to the end, he shall be saved" (Matthew 24:12-13 *NASB*). We must take this verse seriously and be watchful, strengthening ourselves in our Lord Jesus.

Jesus also said, "Behold, I am coming as a thief. Blessed is he who *watches,* and keeps his garments, lest he walk naked and they see his shame" (Revelation 16:15, *Italics added*). The Lord pronounced a special blessing on the person who doesn't allow someone to steal his robe of righteousness and keeps himself pure and holy—morally, financially, and ethically.

Blessed is the person who, in these last days, is full of integrity and love with no guile or deceit. Watch so that no person is used by the enemy to steal your robe of righteousness and you are never guilty of removing the robe of righteousness from another person's life. *Watch and pray!*

17

APPEALING FOR DIVINE INTERVENTION

Many people who experience hopelessness in their prayers believe that, because God is sovereign, everything is predetermined. If everything is predestined, they reason, then prayer becomes useless and hopeless. They base their conclusions on the fact that some things in Scripture are predestined—such as the Russian invasion of Israel predicted in Ezekiel thirty-eight and thirty-nine.

While that event may be predestined, how it affects Israel is not predestined *in detail*. If we ask God to minimize the loss of life, no evidence indicates that our prayers will go unanswered.

If we fail to realize the value of prayer in predestined events, we are given over to a pessimistic world view and filled with cynicism and a distrustful unbelief. We can even begin to believe that God wound up the world like a clock, stepped back, and no longer intervenes in history.

The whole message of prayer, on the contrary, is that God *will* supernaturally intervene in the affairs of life. The Lord is concerned about your son, your family, your pastor, and the Middle East. The good news is that God Himself will intervene in these last days.

In a previous chapter, I discussed how Abraham interceded for Lot when Sodom and Gomorrah were about to be destroyed. You may have a friend in Germany who, if war breaks out in Europe, could escape that terrible war because of your prayers. You may have a relative living in Jerusalem, as I do. Although no one else escapes a disaster or war, that person can escape. Prayer can make a difference even in a predestined event. Prayer creates a "pocket of mercy."

In Numbers 14:21 we read, "But truly, as I live, all the earth shall be filled with the glory of the Lord." Can you see how foolish it is to assume that our prayers are useless when we can claim this verse? The glory of the Lord is going to cover your lost friend, neighbor, or loved one. They may live in Cincinnati or St. Louis, but you can pray Numbers 14:21 for them.

Hope For America

2 Chronicles 7:14 also shows that all things are not predetermined. Most of us are very familiar with this verse:

> If My people who are called by My
> name will humble themselves, and pray

and seek My face, and turn from their wicked ways, then I will hear from heaven, and will forgive their sin and heal their land.

This verse indicates that the United States is not hopeless. God will heal America if we meet the conditions.

What are the conditions? 1) pray; 2) seek His face; 3) turn from our wicked ways. What are the results? 1) He will hear from heaven; 2) He will forgive our sins; 3) He will heal our land.

America is *not* doomed. You say, "It's inevitable . . . our preacher says . . . I heard it on a tape . . . America is doomed to destruction . . . there's no need to pray." *That is blasphemy!* God can and will intervene if any nation will seek His face.

The Book of Jonah teaches that there is hope for a wicked nation that prays. You know the story. Jonah was sent to Nineveh to preach that God's judgment was coming and that in forty days Nineveh would be overthrown. But was the destruction of Nineveh inevitable? Did God refuse to intervene? No! Jonah 3:5-9 says,

So the people of Nineveh believed God, proclaimed a fast, and put on sackcloth, from the greatest to the least of them. Then word came to the king of Nineveh; and he arose from his throne and laid aside his robe, covered himself with sackcloth and sat in ashes. And he caused it to be proclaimed and published throughout Nineveh by the decree of the king and his nobles, saying, "Let neither man nor beast, herd nor flock, taste anything; do not let them eat, or drink water. But let man and beast be covered with sackcloth, and cry mightily to God; yes, let every one turn from his evil way and from the violence that is in his hands. Who can tell if God will turn and relent, and turn away from His fierce anger, so that we may not perish?"

The people of Nineveh had faith. They said, "Who can tell? We might be able to change God's mind." And God did spare them! The Bible says, "God relented from the disaster that He had said He would bring upon them, and He did not do it" (Jonah 3:10).

When God spared Nineveh, Jonah became angry because God made him look like a false prophet. What Jonah prophesied did not come true until a couple of centuries later. But God spared Nineveh at this time because they fasted and prayed. Prayer and fasting move God to change His mind.

A similar passage is found in Joel 2:12-14:

"Now, therefore," says the Lord, "turn to Me with all your heart, with fasting, with weeping, and with mourning." So rend your heart, and not your garments; return to the Lord your God, for He is gracious and merciful, slow to anger, and of great kindness; and He relents from doing harm. Who knows if He will turn and relent, and leave a blessing behind Him?

Why sit around feeling condemned and discouraged? God may turn, relent, and bless you. Prayer causes supernatural intervention in the destiny of individuals and the history of nations. Therefore, as Joel 2:17 says,

> Let the priests, who minister to the Lord, weep between the porch and the altar; let them say, "Spare Your people, O Lord, and do not give Your heritage to reproach, that the nations should rule over them. Why should they say among the peoples, 'Where is their God?' "

We can pray, "Spare Your people. Spare America. Spare Israel." The fact that you can pray according to Scripture for God to spare nations proves that He will intervene in the events of mankind. Habakkuk 3:2 is a very interesting passage:

> O Lord, I have heard Your speech and was afraid; O Lord, revive Your work in

the midst of the years! In the midst of the years make it known; in wrath remember mercy.

Even though everyone else comes under judgment in a church, you do not have to. Although everyone else comes under judgment in a city or a nation, you can escape it. Noah did. God put him on the ark. God *always* has an ark of safety for those who seek Him. You have a perfect right to say, "In wrath *remember mercy.*"

Pockets Of Mercy

Zephaniah 2:1-3 exhorts us to seek God and humble ourselves in order to escape His judgment:

> Gather yourselves together, yes, gather together, O undesirable nation, before the decree is issued, before the day passes like chaff, before the Lord's fierce anger comes upon you, before the day of the Lord's anger comes upon you! Seek the Lord, all you meek of the earth, who have upheld His justice. Seek righteousness, seek humility. It may be that you will be hidden in the day of the Lord's anger.

Notice that the prayer must come before the decree: 1) *before* the decree is issued; 2) *before* the day passes like chaff; 3) *before* the Lord's fierce anger comes upon us; 4) *before* the day of the Lord's anger.

I believe that in the midst of judgment we can find "pockets of mercy." When I first considered this concept, I wondered if it was scriptural. Then, during an appointment with God, I came to the passage in Zephaniah quoted above. The Lord revealed that we can be hidden in the day of His anger. There *is* a hiding place in the midst of the anger of God—a pocket of mercy. Everything is not predestined, inevitable, and hopeless.

Maybe you will find a pocket of mercy. You can pray for your Lot in today's Sodom. You can pray for your son who is overseas in the Armed Forces or your friend captured on an airplane by terrorists. You can say, "Maybe nobody else will get out, but I'm going to trust God and send His angels into the situation."

When I wrote this, many American passengers were being held hostage on a plane in Beirut. It appeared that they would all be killed, so I specifically prayed for God to send His angels. I felt faint while I prayed, as though I was in God's will doing spiritual battle. Now the matter is fully resolved. I recently spoke with John Testrake, the captain of the TWA plane. He confirmed that prayer definitely caused the release of the hostages. This miracle was a direct answer to intercession. These people were placed into a "pocket of mercy" as a direct result of prayer.

I do not believe that anything is inevitable *or* impossible. I believe that the Lord provides pockets of mercy in the midst of judgment, whether that judgment is Satan's or God's.

Malachi 3:17 tells of a separation to come:

> "They shall be Mine," says the Lord of Hosts, "On the day that I make them My jewels. And I will spare them as a man spares his own son who serves him."

God is going to spare a certain group of people. In Luke 21:36, Jesus tells us to "pray always that you may be counted worthy to escape all these things that will come to pass, and to stand before the Son of Man." You can be among those who escape. When judgment falls, God can say of you, "You are just like the diamond in My ring. You are My jewel. I am going to spare you as a father spares his own son."

The Incense Of Heaven

Let's look at the Book of Revelation. Although it is tempting to conclude that scriptural events are unavoidable, there is another side to the question of inevitability. Consider Revelation 8:1-4:

> When He opened the seventh seal, there was silence in heaven for about

214

half an hour. And I saw the seven angels who stand before God, and to them were given seven trumpets. Then another angel, having a golden censer, came and stood at the altar. And he was given much incense, that he should offer it with the prayers of all the saints upon the golden altar which was before the throne. And the smoke of the incense, with the prayers of the saints, ascended before God from the angel's hand.

The seven trumpets mentioned in this passage are terrible judgments upon the earth. But before any one of the seven trumpets can be sounded, the prayers of the saints must first be attended to. The angels cannot release judgment until *every prayer* of believers like you and me has been taken into account. Notice that the prayers of all the saints ascend before God as incense before the golden altar. And the trumpets must line up with the prayers. If fire falls from heaven, it cannot fall on people who have been prayed for—they are protected in a pocket of mercy.

Revelation 5:1,8 says,

And I saw in the right hand of Him who sat on the throne a scroll written inside and on the back, sealed with seven seals. . . . Now when [the Lamb] had taken the scroll, the four living creatures and the twenty-four elders fell down before the Lamb, each having a harp, and golden bowls full of incense, which are the prayers of the saints.

These seven seals loose history to occur. Not only was the book unsealed, but the events written in that book were loosed. And the reason the Lord Jesus was the only one who had the authority to release those seals is that He is the only one who has the authority to control history.

Prayer controls both the destiny of individuals and the history of nations. Prayer must be taken into account before the seals are ever broken and the events of history can take place. What a revelation! Your prayers will affect, positively, the individuals for whom you are praying.

18

DEVELOPING A THANK-FUL SPIRIT

The first chapter of Paul's letter to the Romans contains many terrifying passages. The apostle describes the breakdown of society and the degenerate quality of the Roman Empire. Three times this chapter mentions God's turning the people over to their sin.

Verse twenty-four tells us that "God . . . gave them up to uncleanness." In other words, He said, "If you want to lust, fornicate, and commit adultery, I'll just turn you over to it."

Then the apostle Paul says that God gave them up to vile passions—homosexuality and lesbianism—that which is contrary to nature. (See verse 26.) Again God says, "If you are going to be perverse, I'll turn you over to your perversion." The most terrible chastisement God ever places upon a person is to leave him alone.

Finally, Romans tells us that God turned them over to a reprobate mind. (See Romans 1:28.) The statement is followed by a long list of terrible sins:

Unrighteousness, sexual immorality, wickedness, covetousness, maliciousness; full of envy, murder, strife, deceit, evil-mindedness; they are whisperers, backbiters, haters of God, violent, proud, boasters, inventors of evil things, disobedient to parents, undiscerning, untrustworthy, unloving, unforgiving, unmerciful; who, knowing the righteous judgment of God, that those who practice such things are worthy of death, not only do the same but also approve of those who practice them—Romans 1:29-32.

In other words, the wicked not only do those things but clap their hands for others who exhibit such behavior. These passages describe a completely reprobate state.

The Ungrateful Heart

It is interesting, even surprising, to note where backsliding usually begins. The very first sin, ahead of everything I have already referred to, is found in Romans 1:21: "Although they knew God, they did not glorify Him as God, nor were they thankful."

The first step in getting away from the Lord is *ingratitude*. When we adopt a spirit of complaining, discontent, griping, backbiting, grumbling, and murmuring, we lose our thankfulness and have already taken the first step toward backsliding. That fact should put the fear of God in you and me. It should spur us to make sure that we have a thankful spirit at all times.

If you are not thankful for your job, your nation, your husband, your wife, and all that you have, you are already out of the Spirit. All those bad things in that horrible list of sins begin with being unthankful. *Thankfulness to God is the opposite of backsliding.*

The Bible says much about thankfulness. Philippians 4:6-7 tells us, "Be anxious for nothing, but in everything by prayer and supplication, with thanksgiving, let your requests be made known to God." Then "the peace of God, which surpasses all understanding, will guard your hearts and minds through Christ Jesus."

I used to think this verse simply meant that we should thank God when we have received our prayer request. Now I think the verse means more. It says to let our requests be known "with thanksgiving." In other words, our prayers must have the spirit of gratefulness and thankfulness. Our attitude in coming to God has to be one of love and adoration: "I love You, Lord! I am so thankful for what a wonderful God You are!" In essence, that kind of spirit unlocks the heart of God.

Think on the human level: if your child is appreciative and thankful, you are likely to say, "Man, I'd do anything for this child because he is so appreciative." But if he complains, grumbles, and murmurs, you are more apt to say to yourself, "I'm not sure I want to give him anything else because he is so whiny." In the same way, Paul reminds us in Philippians 4:6 to make sure our attitude and spirit in prayer is one of thankfulness.

In verse eleven of the same chapter, Paul continues:

> Not that I speak in regard to need, for I have learned in whatever state I am, to be content: I know how to be abased, and I know how to abound. Everywhere and in all things I have learned both to be full and to be hungry, both to abound and to suffer need. I can do all things through Christ who strengthens me— Philippians 4:11-13.

We usually take that last sentence out of context. In context, however, the thing for which we require the strength of Christ is learning how to be content in *whatever* state we are. Paul had to *learn* to be thankful and content. You and I are not *naturally* thankful. Our flesh and our souls are naturally full of murmuring and complaining.

Sometimes it's harder to learn how to abound. I know many people who can't handle money. They feel guilty about it and can't enjoy it. Even when they are not selfish in their spending, they aren't content with the fact that God blessed them.

Riches embarrass them. We have to learn, whatever our state, to be content, and in that contentment, to be thankful.

The importance of thankfulness is further illustrated in the story of the cleansing of the ten lepers. Although all ten were healed, only "one of them, when he saw that he was healed, returned, and with a loud voice glorified God, and fell down on his face at His feet, giving Him thanks. And he was a Samaritan" (Luke 17:15-16).

We all need to come back to Jesus every day of our lives and say, "Thank You, Lord Jesus, for cleansing me of the leprosy of sin. I was terminally ill. I was hell-bound, and You cleansed and saved me. I love You so much! Thank You for my salvation."

Unfortunately, we are too often like the other nine lepers. Notice Jesus' reaction. He said, "Were there not ten cleansed? But where are the nine?" (Luke 17:17). Frankly, I think God still gets shocked at our unthankfulness.

The leper incident reveals another important concept: they were all cleansed, but the one who returned received something the other nine did not. They all got rid of their leprosy, but one leper was made whole. The Greek word used here for "well" really means "salvation." (See verse 19.) I believe that nine of them got healed, and one got healed and saved. Because he was thankful, he received something more from God than physical healing. In this instance, he received salvation.

For you, it may be healing, financial blessing, joy, etc. But this is a principle: *The thankful person is always going to receive something that the unthankful person does not receive.*

How much time do you spend thanking God? In your intercession and prayer, how much time do you spend adoring Him, loving Him, and simply saying, "Father, I truly appreciate You"?

Why not start showing your heavenly Father how much you care? Make a special effort to bless Him this week. He will be pleased, and, in turn, you will be blessed!

19

HOW TO PRAY FOR YOUR CITY

When Nebuchadnezzar carried many Israelites into captivity in Babylon, the prophet Jeremiah wrote to the exiled Hebrews, encouraging them to treat the city as if it were their own:

"Thus says the Lord of hosts, the God of Israel, to all the exiles whom I have sent into exile from Jerusalem to Babylon, 'Build houses and live in them; and plant gardens, and eat their produce. Take wives and become the fathers of sons and daughters, and take wives for your sons and give your daughters to husbands, that they may bear sons and daughters; and multiply there and do not decrease. And seek the welfare of the city where I have sent you into exile, and pray to the Lord on its behalf; for in its welfare you will have welfare' "— Jeremiah 29:4-7 *NASB.*

The Israelites to whom this letter was written were living in a city against their will. Perhaps you are living in a city against your will. You may have been transferred, feeling as though you are in exile. On the other hand, you may love your area.

Jeremiah told these people to "build houses and live in them . . . plant gardens, and eat their produce . . . take wives." In other words, he said to put down roots.

Then in verse seven he told the people to "seek the welfare of the city . . . and pray to the Lord on its behalf." The *New King James Version* says, "Seek the peace of the city." You may never have prayed for your city or its government, council, or school boards. Yet what Jeremiah said to these exiles applies to us. Pray for your city. If you can get God's blessing on every aspect of your city, you will partake of the blessing *because your welfare is tied up in the welfare of that city.*

In Jeremiah 29:11 the Lord says, "I have . . . plans for welfare and not for calamity to give you a future and a hope" (*NASB*). Claim that verse. You may not be living where you would like to live. But the Bible teaches that finding God in your situation is the key to victory and happiness. You can count on God because when you call upon Him and pray to Him, He will listen to you. And when you seek Him, you will find Him. (See verses 12-13.) God can make any place livable, but you must find Him in the situation.

Praying Against Principalities

The atmosphere in the air is different over different cities or even different areas of a city. We do a lot of complaining about various governmental authorities in our local governments, but we pray very little for our cities. We may pray for the president and the nation, but we do not pray for the government of the place where we live.

God thinks in terms of cities as well as nations and individuals. He refers to key biblical characters by cities—Jesus of Nazareth, Saul of Tarsus, the City of David, etc. In Matthew 11:20-24, Jesus names six cities by name as to how they responded to the gospel:

> Then He began to reproach the cities in which most of His miracles were done, because they did not repent. "Woe to you, *Chorazin!* Woe to you, *Bethsaida!* For if the miracles had occurred in *Tyre* and *Sidon* which occurred in you, they would have repented long ago in sackcloth and ashes. . . . And you, *Capernaum,* will not be exalted to heaven, will you? You shall descend to Hades; for if the miracles had occurred in *Sodom* which occurred in you, it would have remained to this day"— *NASB, Italics added.*

As a result of their unrepentance, Jesus pronounced woe on the cities.

Jesus wept over another city—Jerusalem:

> And when He approached, He saw the city and wept over it, saying, "If you had known in this day, even you, the things which make for peace! But now they have been hidden from your eyes. For the days shall come upon you when your enemies will throw up a bank before you, and surround you, and hem you in on every side, and will level you to the ground and your children within you, and they will not leave in you one stone upon another, because you did not recognize the time of your visitation"—Luke 19:41-44 *NASB*.

If God has moved you to a city, you are to pray for it. You are there by divine appointment. You can change the spirit and atmosphere of your city and bind the spiritual principalities that influence it.

God once showed me, in a dream, the principality over a specific city. He showed me three spirits that were involved. I went to a church in that area and preached a message, telling the believers what the principalities were. Because of my dream, I knew how to pray for that city. The spirits over that city are confusion/chaos, fighting over money, and fighting over foundations. I did not preach the dream, but I used it to find biblical passages to illustrate my points. Then I preached the scriptures.

Different principalities reside over different areas of every city. Your church should touch all these areas because you are responsible for the city's welfare. That is what God is saying in Jeremiah 29: "Love that city. Build, plant, marry, and pray. Don't try to escape. *Pray* for that city. For in its peace and welfare, you will have peace and welfare." Come on, Christians! *You* are the salt of the earth and the light of your city.

Cities are significant throughout the Bible, which mentions faithful cities and unfaithful cities. Is your city faithful?

Fifteen years ago Beirut was known as the Paris of the Middle East. Given over to debauchery, drunkenness, and fornication, it was a "paradise" of the eastern Mediterranean. But for fifteen years Beirut has been given over to war, strife, and division. Is anyone praying for Beirut?

The amount of prayer for a city would make a difference if we got into a nuclear war. Prayer for a city helps determine how successful our evangelism teams are.

Cities are important to God. Abraham said he was looking for a city whose architect and builder is God. (See Hebrews 11:10.) Somehow Abraham had a revelation of a city not made with human hands. God revealed to Abraham that the consummation of the ages was going to be in a city—the new Jerusalem.

The devil thinks in terms of cities, too. In the Book of Revelation, we find the Antichrist system located in a city. It is called, figuratively, Babylon. Many people think it is Rome, and others think it is Jerusalem. Some even suggest New York City. In any case, Revelation 17:18 states, "And the woman whom you saw is *the great city,* which reigns over the kings of the earth" (*NASB, Italics added*). One great city is going to have worldwide power and reign over the kings of the earth. But that reign will come to a sudden end:

> "Woe, woe, the great city, she who was clothed in fine linen and purple and scarlet, and adorned with gold and precious stones and pearls. . . ." And every shipmaster and every passenger and sailor, and as many as make their living by the sea, stood at a distance, and were crying out . . . weeping and mourning, saying, "Woe, woe, the great city, in which all who had ships at sea became rich by her wealth, for in one hour she has been laid waste"—Revelation 18:16-19 *NASB*.

Some seaport city that controls the entire world will be destroyed in one hour. Every merchant, traveler, and person will grieve—everyone except the saints. Verse twenty says, "Rejoice over her, O heaven, and you saints and apostles and prophets, because God has pronounced judgment for you against her." In the next chapter, they are shouting "Hallelujah" because the city is destroyed.

God also has a city—a "holy city, new Jerusalem, coming down out of heaven from God, made ready as a bride adorned for her husband" (Revelation 21:2 *NASB*). God is centered in the new Jerusalem.

We Christians think of nations and individuals but forget about cities. The Bible says to pray for all those in authority. (See 1 Timothy 2:1-2.) We think of the president, congressional leaders, senators, and representives. But we should include the mayor and the city council. Some city councils are a joke. Many councils and governmental systems have been controlled by ungodly, criminal or religious factions for decades. We need Christians to run for those positions.

More than running for office, though, we must offer prayer and intercession. The Church needs to capture and rule over each city. This is our calling.

Love Your City

You cannot pray for a city unless you love it. Complainers and whiners will never have prayer power. If you hate your city, you must repent.

You have to love more than people. You have to love the *place* where God put you. That may take some choosing and praying, but you must understand that God has assigned you to a certain place.

The Israelites certainly did not like being assigned to Babylon. False prophets said, "You're going to get out. God's going to help you escape." But Jeremiah warned them, "Don't pay attention to those false prophets. You're not going to escape. You're going to be there for seventy years." (See Jeremiah 29.)

You had better get your attitude right and start loving your city. As you pray for your city, love for it will grow inside of you.

You can put God's hand upon your city. I believe that you can lay hands on a city just as you can lay hands on an individual.

A singles bar in our city was located on a highway leading to our church. Many members of our congregation prayed, "Close that place down, God, in the name of Jesus," each time they passed by. When a young person was killed by a drunken driver who obtained his liquor at the bar, the youth's family sued the owners and put them out of business. Did that bar close because of a lawsuit? No. It closed because "salt" and "light" drove past on the way to church. That suit was *how* God did it, but intercession was *why* God did it.

Every city deserves to have Christians living in it who will serve it, bless it, pray for it, lay hands on it, capture it, and rule it for Jesus' sake.

When it goes well with the righteous, the city rejoices, and when the wicked perish, there is glad shouting. By the blessing of the upright a city is exalted, but by the mouth of the wicked it is torn down—Proverbs 11:10-11 *NASB*.

Many cities have been torn down by the mouths of radicals. Your city can be exalted if you will begin every day by blessing it. Bless the mayor, and bless the council. Clip out newspaper articles, hold them up to God, and say, "See this? I bless my city with justice and equity for all people, in the name of Jesus." Do you think the city you live in needs to be exalted? Let's pray for your city right now:

In the name of Jesus, I am righteous today by Christ and His precious Blood. And as a saint of the Most High, I bless the city of (your city). I bless it in the name of Jesus.

Most Christians have failed God in this area of praying for our cities. We have never thought about it. We should remember, though, that Proverbs 28:12 says, "When the righteous triumph, there is great glory, but when the wicked rise, men hide themselves" (*NASB*). We need to triumph on school boards and city councils.

"Scorners set a city aflame, but wise men turn away anger" (Proverbs 29:8 *NASB*).

When the race riots of the 1960's began in Kansas City, Reverend David Gray started the United Prayer Movement. Instead of being a scorner and a troublemaker, this wonderful black leader worked to get all the white people, all the black people, and all the pastors together on their knees.

I have no doubt that because of David Gray's wisdom and love, the rioting, trouble, heartbreak, burning of buildings, etc. was very minimal in our city. Whenever I read this verse, I think of Reverend David Gray.

Anybody can run down, criticize, or tear something apart. Anyone can stir up anger and set aflame passion—or buildings. But a wise man turns away anger, and he does so locally, within his own city.

Possessing Our Cities

Psalm 22:3 says that God inhabits the praises of His people. If you have ever studied that verse, you know that the *New American Standard Bible* rightly translates the Greek: God is "enthroned upon the praises of His people." We can enthrone God over our municipalities if God inhabits and is enthroned on our praises. Every home group can cause God to inhabit their area of a city through intercession and worship.

I love Kansas City because God has called me here. People make fun of Kansas, but I would rather live here than anywhere else. The bread-basket of the world, it is full of beautiful rolling hills. Also, the people are beautiful. You need to have a similar attitude toward the place where God has called you. Don't let anyone run down your city or state.

Following are seven practical steps to cultivating a love for your city.

1. *Develop roots.* That means investing in your city. Invest service, invest time, and maybe run for an office.

2. *Study the history of your city.* If you can discover your city's history, you can find out what needs to be bound. Was the city started with greed? Who lives in your city? What characterizes your city? Each area of your city has a different principality. We need to study the history of our suburbs, also.

3. *Take a tour.* The principle found in Psalm 48:12-13 is good advice for us: "Walk about Zion, and go around her; count her towers; consider her ramparts; go through her palaces; that you may tell it to the next generation" (*NASB*).

4. *Look at everything.* Open your eyes. We need to look at fountains, boulevards, parks, children, schools, flowers, and trees. What does this have to do with prayer? Open your eyes and analyze!

5. *Have compassion on the poor.* We need to have pity on and bless the slum areas and the disenfranchised areas of our city.

6. *Evangelize your neighborhood.* Bless your neighborhood. You cannot even consider your city without thinking about winning souls.

7. *Love and pray for your city.* Jim Croft, in Ft. Lauderdale, is big on the idea of praying for cities. He had a bumper sticker made up: "We love and pray for Ft. Lauderdale." But whether the idea is placed on a bumper sticker or not, it should be written on our hearts. "We love and pray for this city, this metroplex."

This message is the word of the Lord to every believer: He is going to loose prayer for our cities. We can change the spiritual atmosphere of our cities and our country.

I believe that from now on when you pray, you will not think only of the president and national or international crises, such as Central America, the Middle East, and the Supreme Court. You will be thinking of your downtown sectors and your suburbs—or wherever you have been placed by God. If this can become part of your prayer life, you can change the spirit of your area and release revival.

I am excited because I think this is charting new territory for many of you. Will you start placing your city in your prayers?

20

PERSEVERING IN PRAYER

Jesus was a model of prayer to His disciples. They were so thrilled at hearing Him talk to His Father that they asked Him to teach them to pray. John the Baptist taught his disciples, and Peter and the others wanted Jesus to teach them. So He gave them the Lord's Prayer (Luke 11:1-4) and told them a parable about persistence, insistence, and persevering in prayer:

> And He said to them, "Which of you shall have a friend, and go to him at midnight and say to him, 'Friend, lend me three loaves; for a friend of mine has come to me on his journey, and I have nothing to set before him;' and he will answer from within and say, 'Do not trouble me; the door is now shut, and my children are with me in bed; I cannot rise and give to you'? I say to you, though he will not rise and give to him

because he is his friend, yet because of his persistence he will rise and give him as many as he needs.

"And I say to you, ask, and it will be given to you; seek, and you will find; knock, and it will be opened to you. For everyone who asks receives, and he who seeks finds, and to him who knocks it will be opened"—Luke 11:5-10.

The *Amplified* version translates verse eight this way: "Because of his shameless persistence and insistence, he will get up and give him as much as he needs." At first the man refuses, saying, "I'm in bed, and I can't get up and give you anything." But finally, because of his neighbor's shameless persistence and insistence, he gets up and gives him three loaves of bread.

The Lord could have said five loaves or two loaves. What is the significance of the *three loaves*? Those three loaves of bread represent three qualities of a Christian life that every person should have. The first loaf of bread is being born again. If you died today, would you go to heaven?

The second loaf is sanctification connected with water baptism. Water baptism is not just a ritual but a quality decision to bury everything associated with the old life. People who aren't willing to break away from everything ungodly should not be baptized. To sanctify is to *set apart* from sin.

The third loaf of bread is the Baptism in the Holy Spirit. These three loaves of bread are taught over and over in the Bible.

The Old Testament tabernacle consisted of three different areas: the outer court, the inner court, and the holy of holies. Some people today live in the outer court—they receive salvation and live in the outer court. Some people become sanctified and live in the inner court. And some enter into the holy of holies with the Baptism in the Holy Spirit.

In the parable of the sower, even on the good ground, some produced thirtyfold, some sixtyfold, and some one hundredfold. (See Mark 4:2-9.) This relates to three kinds of Christians— the askers, the seekers, and the knockers. Ask and you'll *receive,* seek and you will *find,* knock and the door will be *opened.* After first receiving God and accepting His salvation, you soon realize from your inner hunger that there must be more to Christianity. You become a seeker. You may be seeking the Baptism in the Holy Spirit, and you may be seeking sanctification.

Many people who talk in tongues have never had the second experience of dying to the old life. They don't even know what sanctification is. On the other hand, many people have been sanctified but have never been baptized in the Holy Spirit.

When somebody comes to us and knocks on our door, we ought to have at least three loaves of bread to offer. We ought to be able to tell them how to be saved, how to be sanctified, and how to be baptized in the Holy Spirit. Of course, Christianity involves more than that—bread alone is not a whole meal.

Pray Without Ceasing

After we've received those three loaves of bread, there is another level of prayer: persevering in prayer. This involves calling on God and tiring of apathy, indifference, and lukewarmness. What happens after we are saved, sanctified, and baptized in the Holy Spirit? "How much more will your heavenly Father give the Holy Spirit to those who ask Him?" (Luke 11:13).

After you become a seeker and receive tongues, you get hungry again and say, "There's got to be more than this." You begin knocking. All the seekers say you have it all already. Askers receive, and seekers find; but knockers find heaven's door open to them. And a knocker has things opened up to him that the seeker doesn't find and an asker doesn't receive. These are three different levels of having the Holy Spirit and three different levels of hunger.

Do you want to learn to pray? The Lord says, "Ask and keep on asking, seek and keep on seeking, knock and keep on knocking." Are you hungry today, or are you lukewarm and apathetic? Are you right with God? People who say they are Christians yet are living in willful sin are kidding themselves. Seek God until you get victory in your life. Go to that door, and break it in if you have to.

Jesus spoke a parable to the people "that men always ought to pray and not lose heart" (Luke 18:1). Many Christians are deeply discouraged. They feel like giving up and may even be suicidal. Prayer is the opposite of "losing heart." It is imperative to see that.

This parable concerned a woman and a judge:

"There was in a certain city a judge who did not fear God nor regard man. Now there was a widow in that city; and she came to him, saying, 'Avenge me of my adversary.' And he would not for a while; but afterward he said within himself, 'Though I do not fear God nor regard man, yet because this widow troubles me I will avenge her, lest by her continual coming she weary me.'

"Hear what the unjust judge said. And shall not God avenge His own elect who cry out day and night to Him, though He bears long with them? I tell you that He will avenge them speedily. Nevertheless, when the Son of Man comes, will He really find faith on the earth?"—Luke 18:2-8.

The unrighteous judge was troubled with the woman's "continual coming." But we do not have an unrighteous judge. We have a loving heavenly Father who *wants* us to come to Him continually.

We are to "cry out" to God "day and night." If you've got a problem, you're going to faint and quit unless you learn how to pray continuously. That means you will wake up in the middle of the night and call on the name of the Lord. When you eat your lunch, you will present your prayer request. Go to Him at all hours, crying out in continual, persistent prayer.

The Bible says to pray "without ceasing" (1 Thessalonians 5:17). We have interpreted that as meaning to pray all the time, every moment of the day. Consider that it may also mean perseverance. In other words, don't cease praying for the one who is on dope, divorced, having an affair, or discouraged. Don't give up.

Right before your prayer is answered, Satan will try to get you to throw in the towel. As a pastor, I have noticed that when God is restoring a marriage, a week or ten days before the stray spouse comes to their senses, Satan begins to work on the innocent party. I prayed with a man whose wife returned from deception and sin at the same time the husband was saying, "I'm tired of being humiliated. I'm tired of being the 'Village Idiot.' I'm going to divorce her." Just when God had answered his prayer, Satan was tempting him to stop persevering.

Temptation to quit is evidence that God is working to answer your prayers. Satan knows he had better work on you when things are going against him on the other end. Don't stop praying when you need to be praying the most.

"Do not become sluggish, but imitate those who through faith and patience inherit the promises" (Hebrews 6:12). It takes more than faith to inherit God's promises. It takes faith *plus* endurance.

The Scripture exhorts us, "Therefore do not cast away your confidence, which has great reward. For you have need of endurance, so that after you have done the will of God, you may receive the promise" (Hebrews 10:35-36).

The Lord goes on to say that if anyone shrinks back, His "soul has no pleasure in him" (verse 38). How would you feel if you woke up this morning and God said, "My soul has no pleasure in you"? The Bible clearly warns against giving up!

Our reason for persevering in righteousness, godliness, and prayer isn't because it is easy or we are free of ridicule. We don't persevere because we see results or because of circumstances. We *do* persevere because it is the right thing to do, and we are going to obey the Scripture. Regardless of what others do, say, or think, and regardless of results, we will be obedient.

Ministering Unto God

Romans 12:12 exhorts us to rejoice "in hope, patient in tribulation, continuing steadfastly in prayer."

241

2 Corinthians 4:1 also declares the importance of perseverance: "Therefore, since we have this ministry, as we have received mercy, we do not lose heart."

"Losing heart" is a graphic phrase. It could be translated as "losing excitement and enthusiasm, losing your heart's desire for something."

What "ministry" is Paul talking about? It could be preaching to thousands, leading a Bible study, or being a home group leader. In the previous verse, he says that "we all, with unveiled face, beholding as in a mirror the glory of the Lord, are being transformed into the same image from glory to glory, just as by the Spirit of the Lord" (2 Corinthians 3:18).

The ministry Paul is talking about is ministering unto God—beholding God's glory, being transparent, having an unveiled face, moving from one degree of glory to another, and looking to Jesus. That's a little different than ministering to people.

Ministering to Jesus brings about a relationship. You can solve any problem by concentrating on your relationship with God instead of focusing on the problem. If the Lord is precious to you, and you are talking to Him, you will hear His voice giving direction and encouragement. "They that wait upon the Lord shall renew their strength; they shall mount up with wings as eagles; they shall run, and not be weary; and they shall walk, and not faint" (Isaiah 40:31 *KJV*).

Be like an eagle that soars on the wind of the storm instead of the sparrow, which is knocked flat and splattered by the same storm. Instead of being *under* the circumstances, be *over* the circumstances.

Ministering to God feeds our inner man. "Therefore we do not lose heart. Even though our outward man is perishing, yet the inward man is being renewed day by day" (2 Corinthians 4:16). The real you is not your skin and hair or the shape of your nose, eyes, or mouth. The real you is the inner man who needs spiritual food, and that's where strength and perseverance come in. The inner man is renewed on a daily basis.

In Matthew 17:20, we find one of the greatest verses on persevering in prayer. Jesus said to the disciples,

> "Assuredly, I say to you, if you have faith as a mustard seed, you will say to this mountain, 'Move from here to there,' and it will move; and nothing will be impossible for you."

While I was in the garden tomb in Jerusalem, the guide grabbed some mustard seeds from a little plant and laid one in my hand. It was the smallest speck of a seed. Our faith is like that seed.

Do you have enough faith to forgive that person who has hurt you and to love them instead of retaliating? Can you pray for them or fast one meal a day for them? Do you have enough faith to plant seeds of love? A tiny seed can move a great mountain.

We usually think of the verse that says, "Nothing shall be impossible for God." (See Luke 1:37.) But here Jesus challenges us. Nothing will be impossible for *us* if we take that little speck of faith and plant it. We can all do that. If He had said our faith must be bigger than the mountain, we'd be wiped out. But He said the only thing we need is a speck of faith, and He said to plant it.

Keep on planting seeds of love, faith, and prayer. Keep forgiving and putting your arm around people to encourage them. We look for something big to do, but the Lord says all we need is a tiny speck of faith. That encourages me to persevere in prayer because it gives me something I can do. In this context, I can move a mountain.

Read Matthew 17:20. Meditate on it, and try to memorize it. If you are discouraged about your problems or someone you love, this is your verse. Begin planting little seeds.

Victory In The Garden

We have never really prayed as the Savior prayed. Jesus' prayer in the Garden of Gethsemane was so intense that His sweat pores dripped blood, and an angel had to come from heaven to strengthen Him. (See Luke 22:43-44.) I am convinced that He would have died right there if the

244

angel hadn't helped Him through the grief He felt from looking into that cup. I'm sure Satan wanted a premature death so He couldn't die for our sins.

Jesus saw all the sins that we have committed—all the sins of every age and every continent. Sins on top of sins zeroed in on the cup of death that He had to drink. Sustained by an angel, praying in intensity and perseverance, the Lord Jesus Christ won the victory in the Garden of Gethsemane. That's why He had the ability to persevere and not faint the next day.

There would have been no Calvary without a Gethsemane. Jesus looked into that cup with all its horribleness and prayed His way to victory. That's why He had such peace the next day. That's how He could hang on the cross and say, "Father, forgive them, for they do not know what they do" (Luke 23:34). How did He have that kind of tranquility? He had prayed through the agony and the heartbreak.

The reason we don't take up our cross is because we have skipped the prayer meeting. We faint because we have skipped Gethsemane. We don't have victory over sin because we haven't sweat drops of blood in the garden of prayer. The Lord is our example of perseverance and intensity.

Some people don't believe in praying twice. Jesus went back *three times*. The first two times He said, "Father, if it is possible, let this cup pass from me." The Father said it wasn't possible. Either He went to the cross and died or all people would go to hell. The third time, with blood dripping out of His pores, He said triumphantly, "Not My will, but Yours, be done" (Luke 22:42). He rose to victory right then and there. The next day He walked out the victory.

We try to walk it out without the prayer meeting. We make a quick, simplistic prayer and then wonder why we can't carry through to victory. The deeper we pour out our heart, the more intense our intercession becomes. Then the straighter our walk and more obedient our steps will be.

I used to think I would never quit. I couldn't tolerate quitters. If someone fell, I could understand. But not if they quit. I took pride in the fact that I wasn't a quitter—without recognizing it as pride. Subconsciously, I assumed that the reason I wasn't a quitter was because I was such a strong person.

The Bible says that wherever we lift ourselves up, there we will be abased. (See Matthew 23:12.) So the devil went to work on me until I wanted to quit constantly.

Now I understand that the only reason I was strong was the grace of God. It had nothing to do with my personality. The Bible teaches that we stand by grace. Our strength doesn't come out of our self-righteousness, our attainment, our fortitude, our determination, or *our* strength. When we go through the devil's wringer, we find out that our strength is the Lord's and not our own.

If you feel like quitting and are tired of persevering, God is showing you that you stand only by His grace. Call on Him. You will find strength in the same place that Jesus did—in the garden, in the quiet place, even when your three best friends can't stay awake. When there is nobody else to pray but you, you receive strength in perseverance and intercession. And once you have it, you'll say, "My strength is the Lord."

You therefore, beloved, since you know these things beforehand, *beware lest you also fall from your own steadfastness,* being led away with the error of the wicked; but grow in the grace and knowledge of our Lord and Savior Jesus Christ. To Him be the glory both now and forever. Amen—2 Peter 3:17-18, *Italics added*.

21

ANGELIC INTERVENTION

I have discovered six truths or premises involved in angelic intervention in prayer. For the sake of clarity, I will establish them at the beginning of the chapter and then support them with scripture.

1. *An answer to prayer requires divine intervention.* A prayer cannot be answered unless God, Himself, breaks in and intervenes. The beauty of prayer is that it brings God on the scene.

2. *Whenever God breaks in and changes what is happening, angels are specifically involved.* Every answered prayer has supernatural agents (angels) bringing about the answer.

3. *Angels participate in every aspect of life on the earth, even in what seems to be the normal, mundane activities of men.* Angels are actually working on our behalf. Angelic intervention is not reserved for extraordinary circumstances, such as the birth, temptation, and resurrection of Jesus.

4. *Angels are especially involved in answered prayer.*

5. *Answered prayers control the destiny of individuals and the direction of nations.*

6. *Angels always line up with the purposes of God.* They will not line up with selfish wishes or soulish desires.

We can only receive angelic help when we also line up with the purposes of God. For example, Balaam wanted to receive money to prophesy a curse on Israel—God's people. If the donkey he was riding had not fallen on the ground and hindered Balaam, the "prophet" would have been killed. Balaam was outside of the purpose and will of God. Consequently, he faced angelic opposition rather than angelic help.

The Lord Of Hosts

To understand these premises, we must also grasp three other concepts. The first concept involves *the enormous number of angels that exist.* What is the number of angels given in the Bible? Daniel 7:9-10 is an exciting passage describing the Ancient of Days, the Heavenly Father, delivering the throne over to the Son of Man:

> I watched till thrones were put in place, and the Ancient of Days was seated; His garment was white as snow, and the hair of His head was like pure wool. His throne was a fiery flame, its wheels a burning fire; a fiery stream

issued and came forth from before Him. A thousand thousands ministered to Him; ten thousand times ten thousand stood before Him. The court was seated, and the books were opened.

This scripture says there were "ten thousand times ten thousand," which equals one hundred million angels, plus the thousand thousands. Revelation 5:11 also mentions over one hundred million angels:

> Then I looked, and I heard the voice of many angels around the throne, the living creatures, and the elders; and the number of them was ten thousand times ten thousand, and thousands of thousands.

This would be *at least* one hundred million angels.

According to Jeremiah 33:22, "The host of heaven cannot be numbered." Hebrews 12:22 is a New Testament confirmation: "You have come to Mount Zion and to the city of the living God, the heavenly Jerusalem, to an innumerable company of angels." Therefore, Scripture teaches that the angels are innumerable.

The second concept is that *Jesus is the Lord of Hosts.* The phrase "Lord of Hosts" or "Lord God of Hosts" occurs three hundred times in the Bible. Jesus is the Lord of an army of angelic multitudes.

Hebrews 1:4-6 says Jesus has "become so much better than the angels, as He has by inheritance obtained a more excellent name than they. For to which of the angels did He ever say: '. . . My son . . . ' 'Let all the angels of God worship Him'?"

Even though angels are supernatural beings, they are not the Son of God. They have to worship Jesus.

The third concept is that *angels are unemployed*. The angels are waiting to be called into action. In Emporia, Kansas, a sign in a church says, "Unemployed angels; please pray." The angels are waiting for us to pray. Much more is going on in the heavenly realm than we realize.

For example, in the Garden of Gethsemane, Jesus said, "Put your sword in its place. . . . Or do you think that I cannot now pray to My Father, and He will provide Me with more than twelve legions of angels?" (Matthew 26:52-53).

In Jesus' time, each Roman legion contained a total of 6,600 men. Therefore, twelve legions would include 79,200 angels. The Savior could have called nearly 80,000 angels to prevent His crucifixion. Jesus died for one reason. *He wanted to*. He loves you!

The Old and New Testaments contain almost six hundred passages about angels. In this chapter we will consider seven of them. Hebrews 1:14 is a pivotal one: "Are they not all ministering spirits sent forth to minister for those who will inherit salvation?"

Angels are servants to the Church. This implies that we are greater than the angels because they serve us. The Greek word here for "minister" is the same word translated "deacon" elsewhere in the New Testament. Angels are deacons and exist to serve and help you and me.

This verse says that *all* the angels are ministering spirits. This means that at least 100 million angels exist. Actually, I believe there are trillions of angels—"innumerable angels"—existing to serve us.

Many people do not like to think of angels as "spirits," lest they confuse them with the Holy Spirit. Obviously, angelic beings were created and are on a lesser level than the Holy Spirit. They are called spirits because they do not always exist in a bodily form. Do not stumble at the phrase "ministering spirits." Instead, meditate on the fact that there are trillions of angels waiting to *attend to your prayers.*

Notice, also, the future tense: "for those who *will* inherit salvation." I want to emphasize this. Each one of the innumerable angels are ministers to come to the assistance and aid of every Christian. Angels are servants of the heirs of salvation.

We do a lot of talking about binding demons, but what do we loose? We loose the angels. *We loose angelic help.*

During a worship service, I had a vision. While looking at a family that was having marital problems, I saw an angel of God wrapping the husband

and wife up in his wing—like someone would roll a cigarette. He rolled them together so tightly that nothing else could get into their relationship and they could have no affections for anyone else. Then I saw the angel take his other wing and hold off demonic principalities, powers, and forces.

I stepped to the microphone and began to prophesy this vision. The family did not go through a divorce! Then I began to pray in this manner for eight marriages. In every instance, the marriages were immediately revitalized.

I have seen miracle after miracle when angels are loosed and intervene in people's lives. Remember, since angels are not independently sovereign, they will only do God's will and enforce His purposes. But we can pray and ask God to send an angel to intervene.

Do you know someone who is backslidden? Pray specifically that God will put an angel's wing between that person and his sin, depression, or discouragement. Prayer puts angels in action to intervene in people's lives—at home, in church, on the job, and in school.

Agents For Service

A second key passage is found in John 1:51. Jesus said to Nathanael, "Most assuredly, I say to you, hereafter you shall see heaven open, and the angels of God ascending and descending upon the Son of Man."

Angels always ascend and descend on Jesus. He is the ladder to heaven. An angel will never be released to minister except through the Lord.

Throughout Jesus' public ministry, every time He performed a miracle, angels were the agents who did the work. Although His disciples couldn't see them, angels were working. The Most High rules through angels. Those miracles, the gifts of the Holy Spirit, and so forth, operate in cooperation with angelic activity.

The ladder Jacob saw was the Lord Jesus Christ. (See Genesis 28:12.) When we pray in the Spirit in the name of Jesus, the angels are loosed to minister to the heirs of salvation.

During the storm on the Sea of Galilee, the disciples woke Jesus, crying, "Teacher, do You not care that we are perishing?" (Mark 4:38). Jesus awoke and said, "Peace, be still!" (verse 39). With that word, He calmed the sea. Heaven opened, and Jesus performed the miracle. But undoubtedly the angels were the agents that carried out the order.

An illustration from the Old Testament shows the same principle. Remember the ten plagues God brought against Egypt? When you read the book of Exodus, you have no hint at all that there were any angels around—except the tenth plague, the angel of death. When you read of frogs, lice, flies, the Nile turned to blood, and the darkness, you don't think of angels. However, the Word of God proves that every one of those miracles of judgment were caused by angels.

Psalm 78:42-49 speaks of the plagues God sent. "He cast on them the fierceness of His anger, wrath, indignation, and trouble, by sending angels of destruction among them" (verse 49). The *New American Standard Bible* says, "He sent a band of destroying angels." Therefore, angels were definitely involved in those events.

When Jacob was returning to Israel after spending a number of years in Lebanon (the result of tricking Esau and having to flee for his life), the angels of God met him. (See Genesis 32:1.) Remember, we must line up with God's purposes in order to receive angelic help. Jacob was going back into God's purposes and returning home where he belonged. "When Jacob saw them, he said, 'This is God's camp.' And he called the name of that place Mahanaim" (Genesis 32:2).

Mahanaim means "double camp." Jacob saw one camp on earth—consisting of himself, his four wives, and their children—and another camp in the heavens—made up of the angels of God.

We live totally unaware of the fact that there are two camps. All we think of is the earthly realm. If our eyes were opened as Jacob's were, we would see the second camp.

In 2 Kings, Elisha, the prophet, had his eyes open. He continually warned the king of Israel of the plans of the king of Syria. The Syrian king's servant told him, "Elisha, the prophet . . . tells the king of Israel the words that you speak in your bedroom" (6:12). His access to information was not through electronic devices but by prophecy, words of wisdom, and words of knowledge.

The Syrians figured that if they captured the prophet, they could capture Israel. Therefore, the king of Syria sent horses, chariots, and a great army to surround Dothan, where Elisha was staying. When Elisha's servant woke up in the morning and saw the army surrounding the city, he said to Elisha, "Alas, my master! What shall we do?" Elisha answered, "Do not fear, *for those who are with us are more than those who are with them.*" Then Elisha prayed, "Lord, I pray, open his eyes that he may see." Then the Lord opened the servant's eyes, and he "saw that the mountain was full of horses and chariots of fire all around Elisha" (verses 15-17, *Italics added*).

Elisha's servant gazed into the supernatural realm. Members of the Lord of Hosts' army were there. This is still true today. Angelic beings surround us for our protection and help.

In The Kings Court

In 2 Chronicles 18:18-21, we sit in on a council meeting in the very courts of heaven. Micaiah, a prophet of God, is talking to the king of Israel, and he describes a strategy session between the Lord and all the hosts of heaven:

"Therefore hear the word of the Lord:
I saw the Lord sitting on His throne, and

all the host of heaven standing on His right hand and on His left. And the Lord said, 'Who will persuade Ahab king of Israel to go up, that he may fall at Ramoth Gilead?' And one spoke in this manner, and another spoke in that manner. Then a spirit came forward and stood before the Lord, and said, 'I will persuade him.' The Lord said to him, 'In what way?' So he said, 'I will go out and be a lying spirit in the mouth of all his prophets.' And the Lord said, 'You shall persuade him and also prevail; go out and do so.' ''

The Lord and His angels were talking over His plans—scriptural proof of angelic participation in the destiny of individuals and nations.

Please catch the significance of this passage. God and the angels had a meeting that caused an entire nation to be defeated and another to be victorious. In this council meeting with the angels, heaven determined the outcome of these events *before the events occurred*.

To bring it a little closer to home, let's look at one more key passage: ''Take heed that you do not despise one of these little ones, for I say to you that in heaven their angels always see the face of My Father who is in heaven'' (Matthew 18:10).

This scripture says every child has a guardian angel. This means that angels are watching the normal, everyday happenings in our lives. As they do so, they see the face of God continually. I believe that guardian angels are assigned to protect us throughout our lives.

A principle of biblical interpretation is called the "principle of first mention." If you study the first mention of the atonement, the first mention of pride, or any other issue, you can get tremendous insight.

The first mention of angels in the Bible is to Hagar, Sarai's handmaid. Hagar had been cast out into the desert.

> The Angel of the Lord found her by a spring of water in the wilderness. . . . And he said, "Hagar, Sarai's maid, where have you come from, and where are you going?" And she said, "I am fleeing from the presence of my mistress Sarai." So the Angel of the Lord said to her, "Return to your mistress, and submit yourself under her hand"—Genesis 16:7-9.

Here we find an angel giving direction and guidance to a troubled outcast. To the natural mind, Hagar was a nobody, just a concubine pregnant with Ishmael. And yet, God sent her angelic help.

You would hardly expect the first mention of angels in the Bible to be in regard to Ishmael and Hagar. This passage teaches us that the Lord is concerned for the so-called "nobodies" and is interested in their welfare. An angel of God gave direction and guidance to someone who was in trouble just like you and me.

In Genesis 19, angels destroyed the city of Sodom after leading Lot and his daughters to safety. Angels were involved in providing something as simple as water in Genesis 21:17-19. It was through an angel that Isaac was spared from being slain in Genesis 22:10-18. Angels are involved in every aspect of life.

Angels provided Isaac a wife and Rebecca a husband. (See Genesis 24:7.) Does this inspire you to pray for angelic help for the arrangement of your children's marriages?

An angel of God spoke to Jacob in a dream and told him to place poplar rods in front of breeding animals in Genesis 31. Who would imagine that angels were involved in agricultural breeding practices? Yet, Jacob prospered through their help.

Angels are excited about babies. In Judges 13:3, an angel appeared to the mother of Samson and told her that she would conceive and bear a son. In 1 Samuel 1:11, when Hannah prayed for a baby, she said, "Oh Lord of hosts." She asked for angelic help. And in Genesis 18, angels were present when the Lord told Abraham his wife would have a son.

Scripture is full of events describing angelic involvement. When Jacob was ready to die, he spoke of the angel who had "redeemed [him] from all evil" (Genesis 48:16).

Victory over sin comes from angelic help. Would you like to be redeemed from all evil? Jacob said the angel helped him.

Angels were instrumental in the defeat of Jericho. (See Joshua 5:13-6:2.) Why did the walls of Jericho fall flat? Because God's army was there.

The first church I pastored was a Baptist church whose congregation believed the Bible. A visiting seminary student said that all the Hebrew soldiers marched in syncopation around Jericho and set up such a rhythm that the city walls fell flat. That was his last Sunday to preach at our church!

The Bible says the Commander (that's the Lord Jesus) of the army of heaven appeared to Joshua, and Jericho's walls fell flat by angelic intervention. Joshua asked the Lord whether He was for or against them. The answer was, in essence, "I only line up with God."

An angel will never line up with man; man must line up with God. Pursue the Lord's purposes, and you can expect the army of God to back you up.

Angels In Action

When David defeated Goliath, he said, "But I come to you in the name of the Lord of hosts, the God of the armies of Israel, whom you have defied" (1 Samuel 17:45). David knew the armies of God were on his side and had a revelation about angels. He also had angelic help in defeating Goliath.

"The angel of the Lord encamps all around those who fear Him, and delivers them" (Psalm 34:7). The devil couldn't get to Job because God had a "hedge" around him. (See Job 1:10.) What was the hedge—shrubs? No, the hedge was angels.

Shadrach, Meshach, and Abed-Nego were delivered from the fiery furnace by an angel. King Nebuchadnezzar said, "Blessed be the God of Shadrach, Meshach and Abed-Nego, who sent His Angel and delivered His servant" (Daniel 3:28).

Angels delivered Daniel from the lions' den. "My God sent His angel and shut the lions' mouths, so that they have not hurt me" (Daniel 6:22).

Too often we have overlooked the fact that angels were involved in all these miracles.

Another interesting passage is found in Daniel 4. In this chapter angels are called "watchers."

> "I saw in the visions of my head . . .
> and there was a watcher, a holy one,
> coming down from heaven. He cried
> aloud and said thus: 'Chop down the
> tree and cut off its branches, strip off its
> leaves and scatter its fruit. . . . This deci-
> sion is by the decree of the watchers,
> and the sentence by the word of the holy
> ones' "—Daniel 4:13-17.

This is the passage that initially caused me to study the effect of angels on prayer. We usually think of God decreeing events. Here, the angels are actively involved in the life of Nebuchadnezzar. They are called watchers because they are interested in the events of earth.

Obviously, angels are not independent of God. He is sovereign, and angels can only decree what the Lord instructs. Angels control events, decree events, and watch events that affect both kings and nations.

Angels were an essential part of the ministry of the early Church in the Book of Acts. When Peter was in jail, an angel of God poked him in the ribs to wake him up, opened the jail doors, and released the apostle. He had more trouble getting into the prayer meeting than he did getting out of the jail! (See Acts 12.) The angel also delivered the apostles from jail in Acts chapter five.

Another significant account in the Book of Acts tells about a non-Christian, a Roman centurian, who began to pray. As he prayed, an angel came to answer his prayers. The angel said, "Your prayers and your alms have come up for a memorial before God" (Acts 10:4). This proves that angels intervene directly in reference to people's prayers.

When the apostle Paul found himself in a storm on the Mediterranean Sea, he said,

> "For there stood by me this night an
> angel of the God to whom I belong and
> whom I serve, saying, 'Do not be afraid,

Paul; you must be brought before Caesar; and indeed God has granted you all those who sail with you' ''—Acts 27:23-24.

In answer to prayer, Paul received angelic deliverance.

The Book of Revelation is a drama of angels, with seventy-one references to angels in its twenty-two chapters. An angel dictated the Book of Revelation to John. One hundred million angels sang praise to the Lamb. Four angels were given the power to hurt the earth. An angel sealed the 144,000. An angel responded to the prayers of the saints in Revelation chapter eight. It was an angel who loosed two hundred million Euphratean horsemen. Michael and his angels war against the dragon and his angels. There is tremendous angelic warfare in heaven. (See Revelation 12.)

Angels proclaim three terrible announcements in Revelation 14:6-19. One of them is what happens to those who worship the beast. An angel will bind Satan and throw him into the bottomless pit for a thousand years. (Notice it only takes one angel!)

Angels are the dispensers and administrators of divine benefits. They undertake our defense, regard our safety, and direct our ways. Angels were created by God for the service of the Church. Created with higher knowledge, power, and mobility than men, angels are God's servants who carry out His orders in this world and assist Him in His sovereign control of the universe. Multitudes of angels, indescribable in might, perform the commands of heaven, keeping in contact with everything occurring on earth so they can help control and work out the destinies of both individuals and nations.

During one of our morning worship services, in October of 1984, the Lord gave me the following prophecy:

"For you sow not in the earthly realm, but you sow in the heavenly realm. For the one that praises his God shall reap angelic help, shall reap angelic covering. For the one who is a worshiper draws angels to his assistance. For My angels are worshipers. And they love to hear the praise of their God.

"And so, when you sow in the heavenly realm by praising and worshiping Me, surely angels come and attend. For it is written, 'I inhabit the praises of My people' (Psalm 22:3). Therefore be a worshiper. You are planting in a heavenly field, and you shall reap a heavenly ministry. For it is written that 'My angels are sent as ministering spirits to the heirs of salvation.' If you will worship Me as a church, saith God, angels' wings shall cover your sanctuary, your marriages, your sons, your daughters, and even your well-being.

"Therefore, know this, that you have not yet heard or understood the power of worship and

the power of praise. Be a praiser, saith the Lord, for it causes even you to sow in the heavenly field and to reap angelic ministry and help. Hallelujah!"

As we conclude this chapter, we will examine a final, glorious passage in the gospel of Luke:

> "Whoever confesses Me before men, him the Son of Man also will confess before the angels of God. But he who denies Me before men will be denied before the angels of God"—Luke 12:8-9.

When you receive Christ and confess Him publicly, Jesus literally shouts your name across the corridors of heaven. In effect, He is saying, "This man/woman has switched kingdoms and accepted Me as his/her King. All of you who make up the armies of heaven must now protect, guide, and watch over this person because he/she is Mine!"

If you have never made a public commitment to Jesus, at your very first opportunity eagerly and excitedly run forward in some church or public service and confess Jesus Christ as your personal Lord. When you do this, then the Lord Jesus Christ, Himself, owns you as His, publicly, in heaven. From that point on, the innumerable, supernatural angels will come to your aid, guide your life, assist your marriage, and watch over your children. They will become watchers over your life because you are an heir of salvation.

22

THE BENEFITS OF BLESSING

Any thorough discussion of prayer must include something specific about blessing others. The first of five key points I would like to make on this subject deals with the principle of *impartation*. By pronouncing a blessing on other people or organizations and putting this principle into practice, we can positively affect our relationships.

Numerous Bible passages refer to this principle. Genesis 48:8-9 says,

> Then Israel saw Joseph's sons and said, "Who are these?" And Joseph said to his father, "They are my sons, whom God has given me in this place." And he said, "Please bring them to me, and I will bless them."

Israel's eyesight was poor just prior to his death, but he wanted to lay his hands on his two grandchildren and pronounce a blessing upon them.

While reading this very passage a number of years ago, the Lord said to me, "Don't *read* it—*do it!* I want you to bless your children." I thought, "Lord, what would I bless them with?"

At that time I had one child who was suffering from "preacher-kiditis." Immediately I blessed that child with a hunger for God and a hunger to read the Bible. Another of my children always seemed to be close at hand whenever an accident happened. I blessed that child with a careful spirit. Another child seemed to have sad eyes almost from birth. Concerned about her spirit, I blessed that child with a spirit of joy. Then I blessed another one of my children with an obedient spirit.

The next day, the child who had "preacher-kiditis" was not feeling well and stayed home from school. I went in to check later that morning, and the child was lying across the bed with *Haley's Bible Handbook* and three different translations of the Bible! I imparted the desire for God's Word into that child without nagging, preaching, or saying, "Hey, you are missing out on God. You don't even worship anymore. What's wrong with you?" I did it secretly in the prayer closet, and the child was supernaturally affected for good.

Interestingly, the blessings I prayed for my other three children were also honored by the Lord. The child who was sad is happy today. The child I blessed with an obedient spirit is very obedient, and the accident-proneness has stopped for the child who seemed plagued in that area.

If we can get hold of this principle of impartation, we will have the power to deposit something
in our parents, our neighbor, or that crabby boss.
We can simply pray, "God, please bless him with
a double portion of joy, in the name of Jesus!"

This principle of impartation can also be seen
in Deuteronomy 34:9: "Now Joshua the son of
Nun was full of the spirit of wisdom, for Moses
had laid his hands on him." The Bible says that
Moses imparted something into Joshua through the
laying on of hands.

When I was a Baptist preacher, we had a Vacation Bible School. One of the teachers came up
with the idea of having the pastor come in and
letting all the children ask questions. On the last
day, one little boy raised his hand and asked,
"When you finish a service, why do you always
hold your hand out over the people when you
pray?"

I didn't know why I always did that, so I told
him that was just the way we always did it. Not
until I received the Baptism in the Holy Spirit did
I understand that holding my hands over the
congregation was symbolic of the laying on of
hands. I was imparting a blessing into the spirit
of the people before they went home. As a
Baptist preacher, I had been following the form
without realizing the meaning.

We can observe the principle again in Genesis
twenty-seven, where we find Jacob cheating Esau
out of his blessing. Isaac was about to die, and he

suffered from poor eyesight in his old age. At his mother's prompting, and with her help, Jacob took advantage of his father's condition. He pretended to be Esau in order to get his older brother's blessing. Rebekah prepared the kind of meal Esau would have prepared for his father, and Jacob wore animal skins that his mother had made in order to deceive his father. Esau came in shortly after Isaac blessed Jacob:

> Isaac trembled exceedingly, and said, "Who? Where is the one who hunted game and brought it to me? I ate all of it before you came, and I have blessed him—and indeed he shall be blessed." When Esau heard the words of his father, he cried with an exceedingly great and bitter cry, and said to his father, "Bless me, even me also, O my father!" But he said, "Your brother came in deceit and has taken away your blessing'—Genesis 27:33:35.

This is an amazing passage because even though Jacob received the blessing under false pretenses and Isaac pronounced it under duress, Isaac said, "I can't reverse it. I have blessed him, and indeed, he will be blessed!" This blessing imparted by Isaac was so powerful that it changed the course of history, affecting the destiny of the Arabs and the Israelis. *Whole nations were affected.*

As I read this passage in my quiet time, I closed my Bible in near disbelief that blessings could be this powerful. I was so excited that I came into the staff meeting that day and shared this principle with the whole staff. Then we went into the sanctuary and blessed everyone connected with an area of ministry. The music minister blessed all the people in the music groups, and the youth leader blessed all the youth workers and teenage youth leaders. We blessed home group leaders, secretaries, elders, and deacons.

If Christians have this kind of power in blessing (and the above passage proves it), then we have missed something very important. We have missed a *specialized way to pray* seldom taught to or grasped by the average Christian. We have the power to impart blessings to people that will change them permanently and alter their destiny.

Blessing Verses Cursing

Blessing others is the exact opposite of witchcraft, voodoo, or cursing people. When we think of voodoo, we think of someone sticking needles into a doll made in another person's image, which brings physical pain or a curse upon that person. Of course, voodoo witchcraft is very foreign to most of twentieth century America. But it is very real in some places of South or Central America, where demon possessed people do have satanic power over non-Christians through witchcraft.

Coming a little closer to home, how do we view cursing? If someone "damns" so-and-so, they are saying or imparting to them a curse. Most people curse without thinking about what they are saying. With their words (and words have power), they are actually wishing, praying, and cursing people into hell. I don't know about you, but I do not want to damn anyone to hell!

The next time you are tempted to curse, you can instantly break the habit by saying, "God bless you with eternal salvation." This approach is confirmed in Romans 12:14, which says, "Bless those who persecute you; bless and do not curse."

The nineteenth verse of that same chapter says, "Beloved, do not avenge yourselves, but rather give place to wrath; for it is written, 'Vengeance is Mine, I will repay,' says the Lord." It is interesting that this verse starts with the word, "Beloved." The Lord commands us not to take our own vengeance but to give place to God.

Blessing others is not just a figure of speech or a suggestion. In the Sermon on the Mount, Jesus said,

> "You have heard that it was said, 'You shall love your neighbor and hate your enemy.' But I say to you, love your enemies, bless those who curse you, do good to those that hate you, and pray for those who spitefully use you and persecute you, that you may be the sons

of your Father in heaven; for He makes His sun rise on the evil and on the good, and sends rain on the just and on the unjust. For if you love those who love you, what reward have you? Do not even the tax collectors do the same?"—Matthew 5:43-47.

The Lord Jesus tells us that we are to love our enemies and specifically pronounce a blessing on those who curse us. Is that just hot air from Jesus' lips or a figurative expression? No, we are literally to pronounce a blessing on anyone who "cusses us out."

Years ago I got a flat tire while taking a group of young people home from a meeting, and we were a little late. As I drove up in front of one young lady's house, her father came out of the house in a rage. He stood at the door of my car cursing and screaming oaths at me for about two minutes in front of all the kids.

Fortunately, I remembered the above scripture. When I was about half a block away, I began to say, "My God, I bless him in the name of Jesus to be saved. Bless him with the spirit of reasonableness; bless him to be kind to his daughter; bless him with a sensitive, soft heart instead of a hard heart."

Blessing others isn't just a nice idea. When Jesus says to love your enemies, do good to those who hate you, pray for those who use you, and bless those who curse you, I believe He means that we are to bless them right where they are weak. If we know someone who is about to have a nervous breakdown or has high blood pressure, we can bless him with peace. It works! We can impart something into them, and the Lord will hear because it is a divine command.

We Are The Blessing

We are called to be a blessing: "I will make you a great nation; I will bless you and make your name great; and you shall be a blessing" (Genesis 12:2).

How many of us truly realize that the greatest blessing is in *being* a blessing? According to Galatians, we are the seed of Abraham. That means that the Abrahamic covenant applies to us. To paraphrase, the Lord says, "I will make you a great church. I will bless you and make your name great; and you shall be a blessing. I will bless those who bless you and curse him who curses you. In you all the families in your neighborhood and those you work with shall be blessed." You and I are to be a blessing to our community rather than a curse.

1 Peter 3:8-9 says to "be of one mind, having compassion for one another; love as brothers, be tenderhearted, be courteous; not returning evil for evil or reviling for reviling, but on the contrary blessing."

Don't try to match the world's cuss words, ravings, or put-downs. Instead, pronounce a blessing.

Christians often wonder what their calling is. This verse tells us that we are *called* to return a blessing when people offend us.

Being a blessing keeps our own attitude positive and uplifting. Jesus said in John 7:38, "He that believeth on me, as the scripture hath said, out of his belly shall flow rivers of living water" (*KJV*). Out of one's innermost being will come a flow—rivers of life instead of garbage and junk.

When you bless someone you stay positive. Instead of calling one of your children a rebel, go into your prayer closet and pray, "I bless you with a compliant spirit of submission to authority and a spirit of yielding to the will of God." When you learn to pray this way, you will no longer say, "She is such a grouch." Instead you will say, "I bless her with joy. I bless her with a revelation of Jesus. I bless her with salvation." You stay positive because you are looking to bring forth the good qualities in others instead of focusing on the bad.

A number of contrasting terms will help to illustrate this concept. Consider the following: blesser vs. curser; encourager vs. critic; positive vs. negative; good fruit vs. discouragement; better vs. bitter; prayer vs. murmurer; production vs. stagnation; appreciate vs. depreciate. Most of us will land on one side or the other of each of these pairs of words.

For example, whether we are discussing teenagers, labor unions, the office, or school, there will always be people who specialize in cutting other people down. Some of it is playing around and joking, but the spirit is wrong—it is obviously not the Holy Spirit. A former elder in our church said he once prided himself in being able to cut anybody down in two minutes and make them look like a fool. Unfortunately, we have all been pretty good at cutting people down.

Speaking of good fruit versus discouragement, I am sure that many husbands can recall times when our wives tried to do something, and in cutting them down we ruined their whole effort. Maybe she was trying to bake something nice; but she burned it, and you made fun of her. What was her attitude? "I'd just as well forget it. He doesn't even appreciate the effort. . . ."

The concept of better versus bitter is also interesting. For every situation that happens in life, we either become better or bitter. It all depends on our attitude.

Production versus stagnation is a concept that applies to our personal lives as well as the work world. If we are blessing people, we will increase production in our office, our factory, or in our children. Have you ever seen people stagnated? Have you seen the child, husband, or wife who simply gives up? What about the employee who has thrown in the towel in discouragement or defeat?

I recently talked to a couple of individuals who work for a prestigious firm. They are expected to do quality work but are never complimented for what they do. No one ever says, "I appreciate you" or "You are doing a good job. You are a valuable employee." The only comments they get from the people above them are critical comments. That is a bad spirit.

The word "appreciate" means "to increase in value." We need to tell people we appreciate them. We can actually place something into our boss, our fellow employees, or our family by praying and pronouncing a blessing upon them. When we appreciate a person, we increase their value to us.

A Royal Blessing

This whole topic is so important to God that He Himself gave Moses a blessing that He *ordered* the priests to pronounce on the children of Israel. The Lord wanted His priests to be positive: He wanted them to be "blessers." This blessing, found in Numbers 6:24-27 (*NASB*), should be familiar to you: "The Lord bless you, and keep you." I am sure none of us would be offended if someone blessed us and asked God to keep us this week.

"The Lord make His face to shine upon you." This verse speaks about our countenance and our joy.

"And be gracious to you." We all need all the grace we can get!

"The Lord lift up His countenance on you, and give you peace." This part of the verse is not speaking about our face but His face. This verse

277

literally means, "May He brighten up and smile when He looks out at you."

Although this twenty-seventh verse is not part of the blessing itself, it is an important part of this passage: "So they shall invoke My name on the sons of Israel, and I then will bless them."

God did not say, "I might," "I could," or "I should." He said, "I *will* bless them." When I pronounce this blessing, I always conclude by saying, "In the name of the Messiah, the Lord Jesus Christ."

Blessing others is sometimes like the little girl being attacked by a ferocious dog. She just yells, "MOM!" Sometimes we don't need to go into the details, we just need to yell, "JESUS!" As long as we use the Name, we don't need to always fill in the details. We can simply put "His Name on them."

So, dear reader, I want to pronounce the following blessing and benediction on you:

> "*The Lord bless you, and keep you; the Lord make His face shine on you, and be gracious to you; the Lord lift up His countenance on you, and give you peace. In the name of the Messiah, the Lord Jesus Christ.*"

23

TOUCHING THE HEART OF GOD

Prayer is not a matter of mechanics. Neither can it be reduced to showing up with a list of prayer requests. Prayer enables a believer to know God and fall in love with Him. A relationship between a bride and groom in which the bride shows up with a want-list for her husband is absurd. A bride and groom enjoy a love relationship because they are married.

Christians—the Body of Christ—are God's bride. We need a relationship in which we come to know our Husband's heart. That relationship is developed with prayer, the action that brings intimate interaction between Christ and His bride.

The reason prayers go "weird" is because they become separated from the relationship with God. A relationship will produce revelation, which will produce faith. We receive faith when God speaks a word to us, and that faith produces good fruit.

In contrast, mechanical formulas produce imaginings, and imaginings produce false faith or hyper-faith, which in turn produce weird works. *Webster's New Collegiate Dictionary* defines "weird" thus: "of, relating to, or caused by witchcraft or the supernatural; magical."

Living Relationships

Having an appointment with God each morning can become mechanical. Even when we *are* committed to spending a half hour or hour with God, we can find that we meet the printed pages of our Bible instead of Him. We can go through the motions until our quiet time becomes stagnant and God does not even communicate with us.

Prayer must be a relationship, not a formula. It's not a matter of saying something a thousand times, shouting loud enough, or confessing, "I'm healed!" Too often what we are really thinking is, "I hope I am."

Any problem can be solved by participating in a relationship with God, but if the relationship is not there, that means we've eliminated God and are praying to ourselves. The outcome of a formula or mere mechanics is that something comes into our mind that is not from the Holy Spirit. We have an imagination instead of a revelation. Therefore, the potential arises to have false faith that produces weird behavior instead of fruit.

I believe that all of us at one time or another have missed the mark. Our imaginations have carried us away from Him. We were very sincere, and it's hard to understand how we could have missed it. How did we receive foolish leadership during intercession? We prayed, sought God, and maybe spoke in tongues for two hours. The answer is that it had become *mechanical*. We tried to make it work.

God's arm cannot be twisted unless He allows it to be twisted. You may say, "I've twisted God's arm." I have, too. However, the only reason we talked God into anything is because He let us, knowing we were children. As we grow and mature in the Lord, those days soon fade.

A groom and a bride have a love relationship that is not based on manipulation. Prayer is not manipulating God to work for you. Have you ever known someone who acted like a friend just because they wanted to use you? As it turned out, they didn't like you. They wanted money or favors. I call this *the rape of a friendship*.

Have you ever been invited over to someone's house under the guise of friendship, only to find they wanted to sell you some product? Whether or not the items were quality merchandise is immaterial. When someone uses us, we feel violated, used, and abused.

We do this to God every day. In effect, we are saying, "I don't want You, God. I want You to move for me. I have this list. . . ." But God says, "I want a bride I can hold close to Me."

We think—because we heard a sermon saying that if we stand on the Word and say it often enough and loud enough, without backing down—God will have to comply. But God wants our fellowship and our love. He wants a people who enjoy being with Him. A bride enjoys being with her husband. We will never understand prayer if we do not understand that it cannot be separated from love.

We are born again to be a bride! God, the Father, is going to congratulate Jesus on His bride. He will be happy with the one that Jesus picked out to marry.

The bride is going to be beautiful like Jesus. That says a great deal about the purpose of prayer. How many prayers do we pray about reflecting the beauty of Jesus?

There is no such thing as church growth without bride preparation. A church may grow in numbers, but if there's been no bride preparation, the church hasn't had true growth. A Spirit-filled church consists of people who live right and have a different value system than the world. True church growth is measured by how much the people reflect Jesus.

This is particularly true in the area of moral purity. A bride who is in love with her husband would never commit adultery. We worry so much about who the Antichrist is and who the whore church is. The whore church is comprised of those people who have two husbands, regardless of their denomination. If we go to bed with a different spirit other than the Holy Spirit, we are a spiritual whore, not a member of the bride of Christ.

Writing to believers, James said, "Adulterers and adulteresses! Do you not know that friendship with the world is enmity with God? Whoever therefore wants to be a friend of the world makes himself an enemy of God" (James 4:4).

Concentrate on getting to know Jesus. John 17:3 says, "This is eternal life, that they may *know* You, the only true God, and Jesus Christ whom You have sent" (*Italics added*).

Psalm 42:1-5 is an excellent example of a soul yearning for intimate fellowship with God:

> As the deer pants for the water brooks, so my soul pants for You, O God. My soul thirsts for God, for the living God. When shall I come and appear before God? My tears have been my food day and night, while they continually say to me, "Where is your God?" When I remember these things, I pour out my soul within me. For I used to go with the multitude; I went with them to the house of God, with the voice of joy and praise, with a multitude that kept a pilgrim feast.
>
> Why are you cast down, O my soul? And why are you disquieted within me? Hope in God, for I shall yet praise Him for the help of His countenance.

Let me summarize this: *Relationship* produces *revelation,* which produces *faith,* which produces *good fruit. Mechanical formulas* produce *imaginations,* which produce *false faith,* which produces *weird works.* It is a four-fold progression either way.

Living To Bless God

Instead of attempting to reduce God and His greatness to a formula that twists His arm, we'd be better off if we just said, "I love You."

> O God, You are my God; early will I seek You; my soul thirsts for You; my flesh longs for You . . . I have looked for You in the sanctuary, to see Your power and Your glory. . . . Thus I will bless You while I live—Psalm 63:1-4.

This Psalm describes a relationship of longing for God, looking to see His power and glory, and blessing Him with our lives. So "let us know, let us pursue the knowledge of the Lord. His going forth is established as the morning; He will come to us like the rain, like the latter and former rain to the earth" (Hosea 6:3). Let's press on to know the Lord!

Only those who are in union with God will know His heart. You cannot know an individual's heart unless you are in union with that person.

Union is the exact opposite of surface communication and involves spirit, soul, and body.

Prayer requires an intimate love relationship with God—talking to, clinging to, and trusting God. This relationship is not based on rules, works, how many chapters we read, or how many hours we pray. When our appointments with God are meaningful, we receive revelation as He speaks to us. We touch His Spirit, and He touches our spirit.

We have many substitutes for a relationship with God. Often we copy tapes and preach other people's revelations instead of hearing from God ourselves.

Sometimes you can tell what tapes or books a person has been studying by listening to their prophecies. You can also often tell what denomination or church a person is in—or what part of the country they are from—by listening to them prophesy. Many times we become copy-cats of the latest charismatic leader.

This is not relationship with God. When a "bride" prophesies, it is from the Holy Spirit's revelation, and it is a pure utterance—separate from books, tapes, study, geographic location, or theological streams.

Many times we assume we are being led by God, and we haven't prayed. We haven't heard God's voice. We are simply a *charismatic humanist*. Our concepts are not scriptural but well-sounding sentences coming from human, soulish wisdom.

Without a relationship with God, we are very vulnerable to clever sentences, hyped-up cliches, and religious paths that are far from the Lord's will.

Even soul winning, prayer meetings, and church services are too often religious instead of born of and led by the Holy Spirit. Too many sermons are soulish rather than inspired by God. We must understand that our goal is to develop a *relationship with God.* Out of that relationship we are to live and move and have our being in Him. (See Acts 17:28.)

God is preparing a bride for Jesus—''a glorious church, not having spot or wrinkle or any such thing, but that it should be holy and without blemish'' (Ephesians 5:27).

Jesus is going to present to Himself a glorious Church, a bride without a flaw or a dirty garment. This glorious bride will have a relationship with God that keeps her on the right track and involves intimate communication, holiness, and revelation.

This glorious bride is described in the Song of Solomon: ''How beautiful you are, my darling, how beautiful you are! Your eyes are like doves'' (Song of Solomon 1:15 *NASB*).

The Groom, the Lord Jesus Christ, is going to describe us, His Church, as being His beautiful darling. He is going to be especially impressed with our eyes, because our eyes will be full of light. Our eyes will be like doves, that is, like the Holy Spirit.

Touching the heart of God is much more than our prayers lining up with God's purposes. It means to be Jesus' beautiful bride—pleasing and delightful to Him. It means that Jesus, the heavenly Bridegroom, looks out of heaven, sees your character and your quality of life, and smiles because He is so pleased and delighted. Touching His heart means that we, His Church, are a great source of satisfaction to Jesus.

> But we all, with unveiled face beholding as in a mirror the glory of the Lord, are being transformed into the same image from glory to glory just as from the Lord, the Spirit—2 Corinthians 3:18 *NASB.*

The essence of prayer, then, is to touch God's heart until we reflect the very glory of Jesus Himself.

ABOUT THE AUTHOR

Ernest J. Gruen leads a staff of 75, including ten pastors and a congregation numbering 3,000. Ernie Gruen is on the Executive Board of the *National Leadership Conference* and is a member of the *Network of Christian Ministries.* He is a well-known Bible teacher and is often requested as a seminar speaker.

Pastor Gruen has published three books, the first being *Freedom To Choose,* now in its sixth printing. He graduated with honors from Friends University in Wichita, Kansas, and received his Master of Divinity Degree at the Central Baptist Theological Seminary in Kansas City, Kansas.

Pastor Gruen and his congregation are strongly committed to missions. The church now supports some thirty-two families and projects in more than fifteen countries.

For additional information concerning seminars, please address:

Ernest J. Gruen
Full Faith Church Of Love
6824 Lackman Road
Shawnee, Kansas 66217